TWENTIETH CENTURY DEPTH STUDY

Russia and the USSR: Empire of Revolution

HAMISH MACDONALD

General Editor: Josh Brooman

D1494628

LONGMAN

Contents

Unit 1 • An Empire of contrasts and troubles

1.1 Nicholas Romanov and Lenin: two family tragedies

Source 1

An informal photograph of Tsar Nicholas II (1868–1918) from a collection kept at Windsor by the British royal family. Queen Victoria was the grandmother of his wife, Alexandra. He is reading the *Petersburg News*, the official newspaper which the government carefully censored.

Source 2

A photograph of Vladimir Ilyich Ulyanov (1870–1924), better known by the name he used as a writer and revolutionary, 'Lenin'. This photograph is from the files of the Tsar's secret police, the Okhrana.

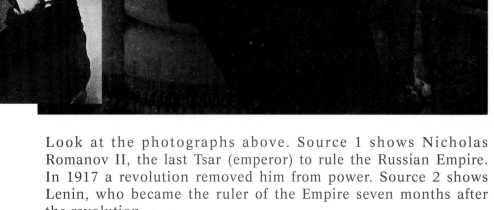

Look at the photographs above. Source 1 shows Nicholas Romanov II, the last Tsar (emperor) to rule the Russian Empire. In 1917 a revolution removed him from power. Source 2 shows Lenin, who became the ruler of the Empire seven months after the revolution.

Both men suffered a family tragedy when they were teenagers. The tragedies had one thing in common – both involved revolutionaries. The first part of this unit describes these tragedies and explains this link. At the end of the unit you should consider the effect the tragedies had on the attitudes of both men to revolutionaries.

■ For what different purposes were the photographs (Sources 1 and 2) taken?

Source 3

An artist's view of the assassination of Alexander II in St Petersburg 1881.

Source 4

The Church of the Saviour on the Spilled Blood, Leningrad.

The death of a grandfather

Look at the picture of the church (Source 4) which was built between 1887 and 1907. It has an unusual name, 'The Church of the Saviour on the Spilled Blood'. Source 3 helps to explain this name. It shows what happened on this spot on 13 March 1881 when Nicholas's grandfather, Tsar Alexander II, rode past in his carriage. A Polish student who was a revolutionary threw a bomb at him.

Nicholas, who was 13 at the time, was brought to see his grandfather dying. A cousin who was also there remembered:

Source 5

Grand Duke Alexander Mikhailovich, *Once a Grand Duke,* 1931. Alexander was Nicholas's cousin, a loyal friend from childhood who also became his brother-in-law. This source is from his autobiography.

The Emperor lay on the couch .... Three doctors were fussing around, but science was obviously helpless .... He presented a terrible sight, his right leg torn off, his left leg shattered, innumerable wounds all over his head and face .... One eye was shut, the other expressionless. I clung to Nicky's arm. He was deathly pale in his blue sailor's suit. His mother, stunned by the catastrophe, was still holding a pair of skates in her trembling hands.

The death of a brother

Nicholas's father, Alexander, became the new Tsar – Alexander III. This tough, ruthless man cracked down on students and on any sign of opposition to his rule. His secret police, the Okhrana, hunted down his enemies. In 1887 they arrested a young man called Alexander Ulyanov who was carrying a bomb which he planned to use to kill the Tsar. Ulyanov was a student at the University of St Petersburg and belonged to a terrorist group called the People's Will. He was given a public trial and hanged with others involved in the plot.

Alexander Ulyanov had a younger brother, Vladimir Ilyich, who later became known as 'Lenin'. Vladimir was born in the town of Simbirsk in 1870. His happy childhood ended when he was 16. First his father, a school inspector, died. Then, in the following year, his brother was tried and hanged. From then on his whole family suffered; the people of Simbirsk avoided contact with the family of an executed terrorist. They moved to Kazan in 1888. Lenin's headmaster, Fedor Kerensky (father of the revolutionary, Alexander Kerensky) helped him get into Kazan University by writing in his report that he:

Source 6

A report from a Russian collection of sources, *Molodaia gvardiia*, 1924.

... neither in school nor out of it gave his superiors or teachers by a single word or deed any cause to form of him an unfavourable opinion.

But from the moment Lenin arrived at university he was seen as the brother of a terrorist. In December the police arrested him for taking part in a demonstration against the university rules. The university expelled him. For the next four years he lived off his mother's pension and studied on his own. In 1890 the University of Kazan allowed him to take his exams as an external student. However, by this time he

Source 7

Richard Pipes, *The Russian Revolution 1890-1919*, 1990. Richard Pipes is Polish by birth. His book gives an unsympathetic interpretation of Lenin and communism in Russia.

... was filled with boundless hatred for those who had cut short his promising career and rejected his family, the tsarist establishment and the 'bourgeoisie' .... He gave little thought to the future, so preoccupied was he ... with smashing the world of the present.

Questions

1 Look at Source 4. What is the link between the name of the church and the event shown in Source 3?

2 What is the link between the word revolutionary and **(i)** the death of Tsar Alexander II, **(ii)** the death of Lenin's brother?

3 How might the causes of the deaths of Nicholas's grandfather and of Lenin's brother explain the difference in their attitude towards revolutionaries?

4 For what different reasons should one not trust Sources 6 and 7?

1.2 Nicholas Romanov's inheritance

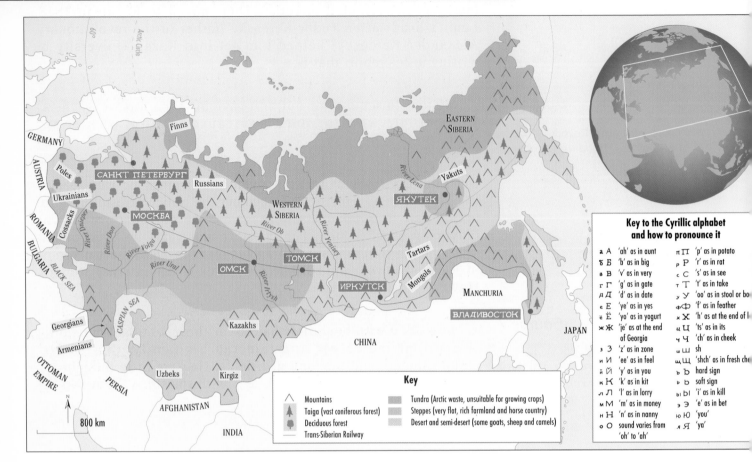

Source 1

The Russian Empire c. 1900. The Empire stretched across two continents, eleven time zones, many different types of climate and five different vegetation zones. Nearly half of Russia is north of 60° latitude on a level with Alaska and Greenland. Winter lasts half the year or more.

Nicholas Romanov became Tsar when his father, Alexander III, died in 1894. He inherited a vast empire (Source 1) of many different peoples, containing rich but mostly underdeveloped resources. The second part of this unit shows how Nicholas felt about his inheritance.

How did Nicholas feel about becoming Tsar?

Here are some of the titles Nicholas II inherited when he became Tsar:

Source 2

K. Fitzlyon and T. Browning, *Before the Revolution*, 1977. These titles were read out when Nicholas was crowned Tsar.

Emperor and Autocrat of all Russia, of Moscow, Kiev, Vladimir and Novgorod; Tsar of Kazan, Astrakhan, Poland, Siberia, Khersones, and Georgia; Prince of Estonia, Grand Duke of Finland and Lithuania; Sovereign of Pskov, Turkestan and the Armenian Regions; Lord and Master of all Northern Countries; Duke of Schleswig-Holstein and Oldenburg and Heir of Norway …

In tears, Nicholas said to his brother-in-law:

Source 3

Grand Duke Alexander Mikhailovich, *Once a Grand Duke*, 1931.

What am I going to do? What is going to happen to me? I am not prepared to be Tsar. I never wanted to become one ... [this is] the worst thing that could have happened to me, the thing I have been dreading all my life.

Being an 'Autocrat' meant that Nicholas did not share power. He made all final decisions and no one could tell him what to do. The law said:

Source 4

From the 'Old Fundamental laws', 1716.

God himself commands that all must bow to his supreme power, not only out of fear but also out of conscience.

Questions

1 How powerful do Sources 1, 2 and 4 suggest that Tsar Nicholas was? Explain your answer.

2 Source 2 shows that Nicholas had different titles for the different countries he ruled. How might this have affected the way the peoples of the Empire felt about him?

3 Use Source 3 to sum up in one sentence how Nicholas felt about becoming Tsar in 1894.

1.3 Why Nicholas dreaded becoming a Tsar

In 1894 the Tsar of Russia was the richest and most powerful man in the world. So why did Nicholas dread becoming Tsar? One reason was that the Empire he inherited presented him with many different problems.

Source 1

The natural resources of the Russian Empire.

What made the Russian Empire difficult to rule?

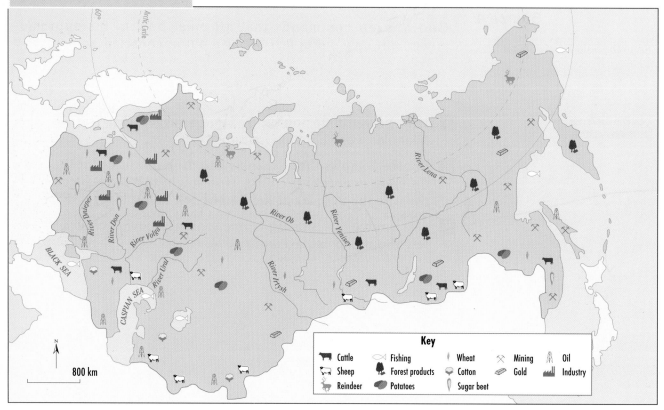

Key

Cattle	Fishing	Wheat	Mining	Oil
Sheep	Forest products	Cotton	Gold	Industry
Reindeer	Potatoes	Sugar beet		

Source 2

The Empire's percentage share of the world manufactures in 1913, League of Nations, *Industrialisation and World Trade*, 1945.

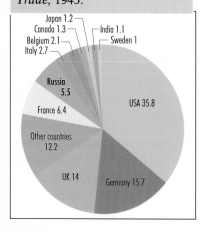

Japan 1.2
Canada 1.3
Belgium 2.1
Italy 2.7
India 1.1
Sweden 1
Russia 5.5
France 6.4
Other countries 12.2
UK 14
Germany 15.7
USA 35.8

The economy

Source 1 shows that the Russian Empire was rich in natural resources. Yet, as Source 2 shows, Russia made less from these resources than much smaller countries.

Russia's main source of wealth was farming. However, old-fashioned farming methods and bad weather often spoiled harvests and caused terrible famines. Farming did not produce enough money to buy new machinery. On the other hand, the natural resources and cheap labour encouraged foreigners to set up new industries and businesses in the Russian Empire. These foreigners took the profits, which meant that Russia had to borrow large amounts of money from other richer countries such as France, for building projects like the Trans-Siberian Railway.

Distance and communications

The size of the Russian Empire made it difficult to rule. Nicholas's Empire covered a sixth of the world's surface and was over twice the size of the United States. It stretched from Europe in the west

Source 3

Forests, mountains and deserts made up large parts of the Russian Empire. The great coniferous forest (*taiga*) is the largest in the world stretching from Scandinavia in the west to the sea of Okhotsk in the east. Most of the country is flat. The Ural Mountains rise no higher than 1,900 metres. High mountains are found on the fringes of the country.

Source 4

This pie chart based on the first Russian census taken in 1897, shows the percentage of Russian people belonging to the different nationalities.

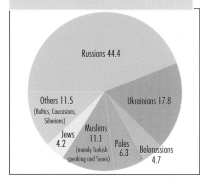

Russians 44.4
Ukrainians 17.8
Others 11.5 (Baltics, Caucasians, Siberians)
Muslims 11.1 (mainly Turkish speaking and Sunni)
Poles 6.3
Belorussians 4.7
Jews 4.2

across Asia to the east, and from the Arctic Ocean in the north to Iran and Afghanistan in the south.

Communications were poor and very slow. There were vast distances to travel. For parts of the year the seas and lakes in the north were frozen. Roads were in a terrible condition, especially in winter. Even on the new Trans-Siberian Railway a journey of 2,400 kilometres from St Petersburg to the Urals took about three and a half days. Today, a train journey to Vladivostok on the Pacific takes over a week. Varieties of landscape, vegetation, climate, and the many different languages spoken were additional obstacles to movement and communication.

A variety of peoples

There were over 125 million people in the Russian Empire and the population was growing fast. The Russians were outnumbered by a variety of peoples who spoke different languages and who differed in colour, in the way they dressed, and in their religion and way of life. Instead of feeling part of one nation, they were divided into over 100 separate nationalities (Source 4).

Source 5

Kirghiz nomads. From Sergei Mikhailovich Prokudin-Gorskii, *Photographs for the Tsar*, 1909. Part of a collection taken specially for the Tsar. Nicholas was so delighted with the pictures that he wanted them shown in schools.

Source 6

The shanty of a settler. One of the first colour photographs ever taken. From Sergei Mikhailovich Prokudin-Gorskii, *Photographs for the Tsar*, 1909.

Source 7

These statistics come from the Russian census of 1897.

A backward society

The peoples of the Empire divided into social classes:

1 Ruling class – the royal family and members of the government	0.5%
2 Upper class – nobles, church leaders, military officers, top civil servants	12.0%
3 Commercial class – bankers, merchants, factory owners, shopkeepers	1.5%
4 Working class – factory workers, street traders	4.0%
5 Peasants – workers who farmed in the countryside	82.0%

Between 1881 and 1900 a large number of peasants moved into Russia's main cities to escape famine and to look for jobs in new and expanding industries:

Source 8

M. Lynch, *Reaction and Revolutions: Russia 1881–1924*, 1992.

Population growth in Russia's main cities, 1881–1900

	St Petersburg	Moscow
1881	928,000	753,500
1890	1,033,600	1,038,600
1897	1,264,600	1,174,000
1900	1,439,600	1,345,000

Low wages and a shortage of housing led to terrible living conditions. It was normal to work eleven and a half hours a day and to return to live in rented rooms like that in Source 9. Up to ten people shared such rooms, the curtain providing the only kind of privacy.

Source 9

A boarding house in
Moscow in 1911.

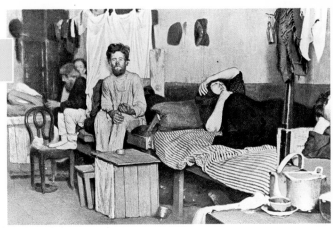

In 1881 very few of these people could read or write. Few went
to school compared with other countries:

Source 10

M.G. Mulhall *Dictionary of
Statistics*, 1884.

Adults able to write in different countries in 1881

	% of adults able to write	% of total population at school
England	84	15
France	78	13
Germany	94	17
Austria	49	9
Italy	41	8
Spain and Portugal	34	5
Russia	11	2

The threat of revolution

In 1891–1892 there was a famine in the Volga region. Lenin, who
lived there at the time, refused to do anything to help the victims.
He wanted the famine to force more peasants to leave the
countryside and move into cities like St Petersburg and Moscow
where terrible working and living conditions would turn them
against the Tsar.

In St Petersburg Lenin and other revolutionaries, like
Nadezhda Krupskaya, ran classes to teach former peasants to
read and write. It was a good way of spreading ideas about
revolution. This was how Krupskaya met Lenin and became his
best friend. It was dangerous work. Krupskaya remembers:

Source 11

N.S. Krupskaya, *Memories of
Lenin*, 1930. Krupskaya married
Lenin in order to be allowed to
join him in exile in 1898. Her
book leaves out moments when
she criticised Lenin and says very
little about herself and her role as
a revolutionary.

Of all our group Vladimir Ilyich [Lenin] was the best equipped
for conspiratorial work. He knew all the through courtyards,
and was a skilled hand at giving police-spies the slip. He taught
us how to write in books with invisible ink, or by the dot
method; how to make secret signs ....

Nevertheless, Lenin was arrested in 1895 for trying to stir
workers to strike and, after a year in prison, sent into exile in
Siberia from 1897–1900.

Questions

1 Use Source 7 to make your own pie chart.
  a Convert the percentage figures into degrees by multiplying each by 3.6. The new figures should add up to a total of 360.
  b Use a protractor to measure and draw the angles. Label and use a different colour for each of the segments.
  c From which segment of the pie would Nicholas have most to fear if he upset the people?

2 In pairs, study Sources 1 to 11. On poster paper, prepare a visual aid to illustrate a talk on the problems which made the Russian Empire difficult to rule. (Some suggestions: lists of key points organised under headings; cartoons with key points in speech bubbles; a labelled map; a spider diagram.)

1.4   Enemies of the Tsar

Once, at the dinner table, Tsar Nicholas turned on someone who used the word, 'intelligentsia'. He said:

Source 1

From *The Memoirs of Count Witte*, 1912. Sergei Witte was Minister of Communications and Minister of Finance.

How I detest that word! I wish I could order the Academy to strike it from the Russian dictionary.

The intelligentsia were the thinkers, writers and artists of the Empire. Nicholas believed that these people were his enemies. This section shows that Nicholas did indeed have reason to fear the intelligentsia, and asks you to consider which of them presented the greatest threat to his position.

Who were the Tsar's most dangerous enemies?

There were two main kinds of intelligentsia: liberals and revolutionaries.

Liberals

The liberals wanted to replace autocracy (rule by one person) with democracy (rule by the people). They wanted a constitution and a parliament (Duma). While some wanted a constitutional monarchy as in Britain, others wanted an elected president as in France or in the United States. In 1905 the liberals formed two main political groups: the Octobrists and the Kadet (Constitutional Democratic) Party.

Socialist Revolutionaries

Most revolutionaries were university students or students who had dropped out of their courses. In 1874 hundreds of students left their studies to go into the countryside to work among the peasants (*narod*). These *narodniks* were Russia's first 'Socialist Revolutionaries'. Their aim was to stir the peasants into violent revolution against the Tsar. But when the *narodniks* tried to talk with the peasants they were often surprised. Their loyalty to the Tsar astonished them. One *narodnik* remembered a peasant saying:

Source 2

O.V. Aptekman, *Memoirs*, 1924. Aptekman was a Socialist Revolutionary who wrote propaganda for the party.

As far as the land goes, we've got little. No place to put a chicken. But the Tsar will give .... We will get the land ! Ab-so-lute-ly! You will see.

Peasants were suspicious of the *narodniks*. Few peasants could understand them; many were afraid of what could happen if they were seen even to talk to them about politics. The peasants' attitude shocked and disappointed the *narodniks*. One of them, Vera Figner, wrote:

Source 3

Vera Figner, quoted in B. Engel, *Five Sisters: Women against the Tsar*, 1977. Vera Figner was studying to be a doctor before deciding to join the People's Will.

My past experience had convinced me that the only way to change the existing order was by force. If any group in our society could have shown me a path other than violence, perhaps I would have followed it ... But as you know, we don't have a free press in our country, and so ideas cannot be spread by the written word. And so I concluded that violence was the only solution. I could not follow the peaceful path.

In 1879 Vera Figner joined the People's Will, the group which assassinated the Tsar in 1881 (see page 4). They hoped that the assassination would encourage peasants to follow their example. However, violence had the opposite effect. The secret police, the Okhrana, ruthlessly hunted down the Socialist Revolutionaries. Universities lost their independence and were put under the control of the Minister of Education. A state inspector with the powers of a policeman was put in charge of student discipline. All student organisations became illegal.

Vera Zasulich, a revolutionary famous for shooting the Governor of St Petersburg in 1878, decided in 1892 that:

Source 4

Vera Zasulich, quoted in J. Bergman, *Vera Zasulich, A Biography*, 1983.

The example of terrorist exploits can impress only those already possessing revolutionary spirit .... But terrorist acts cannot make a movement more powerful no matter how popular they may be.

Marxist revolutionaries

Georgii Plekhanov was one of several Socialist Revolutionaries who broke away from the People's Will. In 1898 he formed the Social Democratic Party which he based on the ideas of Karl Marx. Marx had written:

Source 5

Karl Marx, *Manifesto of the Communist Party*, 1848. Karl Marx (1818–1883) was a German revolutionary whose ideas about history and economics inspired the major communist revolutions of the twentieth century.

The Workers have nothing to lose but their chains. They have a world to gain. Workers of the world, unite.

Source 6

A poster made in 1901 which shows how Marxists saw Russian society.

Plekhanov believed it was important to wait until enough peasants had become industrial workers to support a revolution. Meanwhile, the industrial workers should help people from the middle classes, like doctors, lawyers and teachers, to get into power first. The Social Democratic Party should encourage as many people to join as possible and make friends in other parties. One party member, however, strongly disagreed – Lenin.

Lenin, Bolsheviks and Mensheviks

Lenin argued against the workers helping the middle classes get into power first. He saw clearly that most Russians were peasant farmers who owned land and wanted more. However, an increasing number of peasants were becoming industrial workers. He thought that a well-disciplined party of professional

Source 7

A religious procession in Kursk province. The artist Ilya Repin painted this in 1882 soon after the assassination of Alexander II.

revolutionaries should take power for them.

Most of the party disagreed with Lenin. At a meeting of the party in London in 1903 a vote was taken which Lenin claimed won him the argument. His supporters took the name 'Bolsheviks', which means 'the majority'; they incorrectly labelled Plekhanov's supporters 'Mensheviks', which means 'the minority'.

Artists and propagandists

Among the intelligentsia were writers and artists who had their own ways of trying to change Russian society. The picture above (Source 7) is an example of how one artist tried to show the tensions in the social life of the countryside. He belonged to a group of artists nicknamed the 'Wanderers' who exhibited their paintings in a travelling exhibition which toured the Empire.

Questions

1 Why did Tsar Nicholas fear both liberals and revolutionaries?

2 Read Source 3. How does it help explain why some Socialist Revolutionaries became terrorists?

3 Why did the Social Democratic Party split into the Bolsheviks and Mensheviks?

4 How does Source 6 help to explain what Source 7 shows?

5 **a** Identify the following groups in Repin's painting (Source 7): important people; soldiers protecting the important people; priests, and servants; poor peasants.
   b What different information does the artist give about each of these groups by their position in the painting, the expression on their faces and their clothes?

1.5 Joseph Stalin: the making of a revolutionary

This section is about a revolutionary from Georgia who would one day become the ruler of the entire Russian Empire: Joseph Stalin.

Why did Stalin become a revolutionary?

Georgia became a part of the Russian Empire in 1801. Georgian is a different language from Russian and has a different alphabet. In the Georgian town of Gori on 21 December 1879 a peasant woman gave birth to a son named Joseph Vissarionovich Djugashvili. The father was a drunken cobbler who beat both his wife and his son.

Joseph's cleverness helped him survive a tough childhood of poverty. Luck saved him from dying from smallpox, which nevertheless scarred his face, and from blood-poisoning, which caused his left arm to be partly withered. His childhood friend remembered:

Source 1

Joseph Iremashvili, quoted in Robert C. Tucker, *Stalin as Revolutionary: 1879–1929*, 1974.

To gain a victory and be feared was triumph for him. He was devoted to only one person – his mother ... he was a good friend so long as one submitted to his imperious will.

At school he was a star pupil. He quickly learned Russian, which he spoke with a strong Georgian accent, and came top of the class. He won a scholarship to train as a priest in Tbilisi but did not like the discipline and attitude of his teachers:

Source 2

A report on Stalin's behaviour by a priest at the seminary.

Djugashvili is rude and disrespectful of persons in authority and systematically fails to bow to one of the teachers ... reprimanded. Confined to the cell for five hours.

Such treatment made him more of a rebel. A fellow student remembers:

Source 3

Joseph Iremashvili, quoted in Robert C. Tucker, *Stalin as revolutionary: 1879–1929*, 1974.

Secretly, during classes, services and sermons we read 'our books'. The Bible was open on our desk, but on our laps we held Darwin, Marx, Plekhanov or Lenin.

By 1902 he was recorded in the Okhrana file on him as an 'active and very serious' revolutionary.

Lenin once wrote:

Source 4

The Writings of Lenin, 1902.

It is necessary to prepare men who devote to the revolution not only their free evenings, but their entire lives.

Djugashvili fitted this description well. He changed his name to

Source 5

A photograph of Stalin from the secret police file after his arrest in April 1902. He then used the name 'Koba'.

'Stalin', which means 'man of steel', and helped organise terrorist activities and bank robberies to get money for Lenin's party, the Bolsheviks. Between 1902 and 1913 he was arrested eight times, exiled to Siberia seven times and each time escaped. The death of his first wife hardened him:

Source 6

Quoted in Robert C. Tucker, *Stalin as Revolutionary: 1879–1929*, 1974

This creature softened my heart of stone. She died and with her my last warm feelings for people.

By 1912 Stalin was one of the Bolsheviks' six top leaders.

Questions

1 Read Source 4. In what ways do the other sources in this section suggest that Stalin fitted this description well?

2 How may each of the following help explain why Stalin became a revolutionary?
(i) Stalin came from a poor family.
(ii) Georgia was ruled by Russia.
(iii) The Russian Orthodox Church was biased towards the Russian way of life.
(iv) The writings of Marx and Lenin.
(v) Stalin's character.

Review

1 a Use the sources and information in Unit 1 (pages 3–17) to describe the changes you would see and experience on the two journeys shown on the map below:
(i) a journey on the Trans-Siberian railway from Moscow to Vladivostok.
(ii) a journey by hot air balloon from the Tundra to the Aral Sea.
b What differences between the two journeys would you expect to notice in climate, landscape and vegetation, people and their way of life?

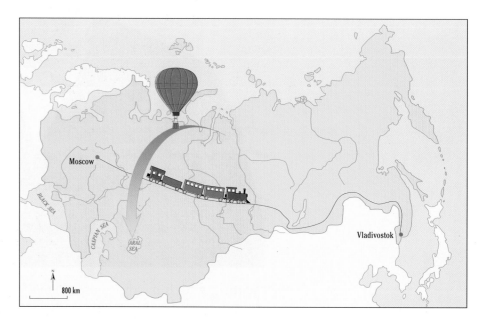

2 Divide a page into two columns with the headings as shown below. Use the information and evidence in this unit to suggest answers to the question at the top of each column.

What did Tsar Nicholas need to do to keep control of the Russian Empire?	What difficulties did Lenin need to overcome to lead his Bolshevik party to power?
Example: Build more railways and good roads.	The power of the Tsar.

Unit 2 • 1905: revolution or dress rehearsal?

A woman worker surrounded by bayonets. The banner she carries reads "Freedom".

Between 1896 and 1905 there was growing pressure on Tsar Nicholas to give up being an autocrat and change the way he ruled the Empire. Nicholas stubbornly refused to do either. In 1905 there was a revolution which finally forced him to allow elections to a Duma (parliament) and to promise more changes. Unit 2 explains why there was a revolution in 1905 and how Nicholas survived to continue as Tsar.

2.1 How Tsar Nicholas ruled the Empire

It was impossible for Nicholas to rule 126 million people alone. He therefore appointed ministers to look after such things as communications, finance and the defence of the Empire. But these men did not work as a team; they worked separately for the Tsar. Often Nicholas gave important jobs like these to members of his family and to friends in the royal court.

Nicholas usually took the advice of the Tsarina – his unpopular German wife, Alexandra. It was said that she believed the Russian people needed and loved 'the feel of the whip'.

There was no Prime Minister but the most powerful minister was the Minister of the Interior. It was his job to keep law and order and to run the Tsar's secret security police, the Okhrana. The Okhrana did not have to obey the law.

Nicholas made all the big decisions himself and hundreds of civil servants carried them out. There were twelve ranks of civil servants, all nobles. Promotion depended on loyalty and

Source 1

A cartoon of Pobedonostsev holding Tsar Nicholas. It is made to look like a religious painting, but notice the skulls around the frame and the whip in Nicholas's hand.

Source 2

The Memoirs of Count Witte, 1912. Tsar Alexander III made Count Witte Minister of Finance in 1892 but Tsar Nicholas and the Tsarina so disliked him that they sacked him in 1903.

Source 3

The Memoirs of Count Witte, 1912. Witte believed Trepov and Plehve had plotted against him.

Zhidy
An unpleasant word for 'Jews'.

Source 4

The Memoirs of Count Witte, 1912.

favouritism, although Jews needed specific qualifications, as did those applying for the top jobs.

Russia had the biggest peace-time army in the world: 2.6 million men – nearly equal to the armies of Germany and Austria-Hungary put together. This huge army helped the police keep law and order.

The Russian Orthodox Church did everything it could to make people loyal to the government. Priests helped to keep law and order and taught that it was a sin to go against the Tsar. The Church's version of Christianity was the official religion of the Empire. Priests taught children that the Jews had killed Jesus.

Nicholas's first top adviser was his old tutor, Pobedonostsev, who was also an important leader of the Russian Orthodox Church. He advised Nicholas never to give up his autocratic rule.

Was Tsar Nicholas a good ruler?

Count Witte, an important government minister, thought that Nicholas was:

> A ruler who cannot be trusted, who approves today what he will reject tomorrow, is incapable of steering the ship of state into a quiet harbour. His outstanding failing is his sad lack of willpower. Though he means well and is not unintelligent, this shortcoming disqualifies him totally as the unlimited autocratic ruler of the Russian people.

Witte also said that Nicholas chose poor advisers:

> The Emperor was surrounded by Jew-haters such as Trepov, Plehve.... As for his personal attitude toward the Jews I recall that whenever I drew his attention to the fact that the anti-Jewish riots could not be tolerated, he either was silent or remarked: 'But it is they themselves, the *zhidy** that are to blame'.

Many people thought Tsar Nicholas insensitive. During the celebrations of his coronation in 1896 he provided free food and drink on the field of Khodynka in Moscow. There, 1,389 people were either crushed, trampled or suffocated to death in a mad rush to get souvenir coronation mugs. Count Witte remembers:

> ... A gorgeous evening party was scheduled for the same day, to be given by the French Ambassador, Marquis de Montebello. We expected that the party would be called off, because of the Khodynka disaster. Nevertheless, it took place, as if nothing had happened, and the ball was opened by their Majesties dancing a quadrille.

Questions

1 Draw a labelled diagram to show who helped Tsar Nicholas rule the Empire. By each person or group of people describe one weakness or criticism.

2 Which personal qualities did Count Witte believe disqualified Nicholas as ruler of the Russian people (Sources 2, 3 and 4)?

3 Look at Sources 2, 3 and 4. Why is it not safe to trust the evidence of Witte's memoirs?

2.2 The causes of the 1905 revolution

In 1905 liberals, revolutionaries, industrial workers and peasants united in a revolution against Tsar Nicholas. The second part of this unit examines two events which together helped cause the revolution: defeat in war by Japan and a massacre known as 'Bloody Sunday'. It asks you to decide which was the most important event. Which one triggered the revolution?

Background to revolution 1896–1905

Student strikes

Leon Trotsky played a leading part in the 1905 revolution. He came from a Jewish family in Southern Ukraine where his father was a farmer. While he was a student he became a Marxist revolutionary. He remembered:

Source 1

Leon Trotsky, *My Life,* 1929. In 1898 Trotsky was arrested and exiled to Siberia. He escaped and joined Lenin in London in 1902.

In 1896, the famous weavers strike broke out in St Petersburg. This put new life into the intelligentsia. The students gained courage .... Some of them had been expelled from universities. In February, 1897, a woman student, Vetrova, burned herself to death in the Peter-Paul fortress [a prison used for revolutionaries]. This tragedy, which has never been fully explained, stirred everyone deeply. Disturbances took place in university cities; arrests and banishment became more frequent.

■ Read Source 1. Who does Trotsky say took part in the disturbances in 1896 and 1897?

In 1899 and 1900 students went on strike in universities all over Russia. In St Petersburg police tried to control them with whips. Students shot and killed first the Minister of Education in 1901, and then the Minister of the Interior in 1902.

The unpopular policies of Plehve

The Tsar chose Viacheslev Plehve to be his next Minister of the Interior. Plehve had helped run the Tsar's secret police (Okhrana) and was well known for his hatred of Jews. He claimed that 40 per cent of revolutionaries were Jews and that almost all revolutionaries were students. He did nothing to stop vicious pogroms (attacks by mobs) on Jews and their property (Source 2).

It was illegal for workers to set up trade unions. Plehve and the Okhrana deliberately set up trade unions to trap revolutionaries.

Source 2

Victims of an anti-Jewish pogrom.

■ What does Tsar Nicholas's decision to choose Plehve as his Minister of the Interior suggest about Nicholas?

A priest called Father George Gapon was an Okhrana agent. His trade union, the Assembly of Russian Factory and Plant Workers, became one of the most popular in St Petersburg. This confused and upset many businessmen and employers who worried that it could lead to trouble.

In 1864 Alexander II had set up district councils (*zemstva*) in the countryside. Peasants could vote in elections to the *zemstva*. Tsar Alexander III had reduced the power of the *zemstva* following the assassination of his father. Nicholas made further changes in 1900 by taking away some of their power to raise taxes. Plehve made things worse by trying to take them over and make them a part of the Ministry of the Interior.

Plehve's unpopular policies upset both liberals and revolutionaries so much that in July 1903 they agreed to work together against the government. They met in Switzerland where they formed a Union of Liberation. On 14 July 1904 a Socialist Revolutionary threw a bomb at Plehve's carriage. Source 3 shows the result.

Source 3

The remains of Plehve's body after the bomb exploded.

■ What different motives did Plehve's enemies have for wanting to kill him?

The Union of Liberation

The *zemstva* proposed that Russia should have an elected Duma (parliament) and a constitution. The Union of Liberation organised a campaign of nationwide banquets to spread the news. However, Nicholas refused to have elected representatives in the government, even just to advise him:

Source 4

The Memoirs of Count Witte, 1912.

I shall never, under any circumstances, agree to a representative form of government because I consider it harmful to the people whom God has entrusted to my care.

The trigger – war with Japan or Bloody Sunday?

The Russo-Japanese war

In 1904 Russia blundered into a war with Japan. Count Witte blamed Nicholas:

Source 5

The Memoirs of Count Witte, 1912.

> … he alone is to be blamed for that most unhappy war, if indeed it is possible to condemn a man who is responsible for his deeds to none but God.

Critics blamed Witte as much as Tsar Nicholas for causing the war. Witte, the Minister of Finance, wanted to use his Trans-Siberian Railway project to increase Russian trade and influence in the Far East. This led to fierce competition with Japan. Nicholas sacked him in 1903.

Japan was a growing power in the Far East with a large navy in the Pacific. Japanese businessmen wanted raw materials for her new industries and markets for their products in Asia.

In 1903 the Japanese had wanted to do a deal with Russia. They would let Russia have a free hand in Manchuria if Russia, like Britain, gave Japan a free hand in Korea. However, wealthy Russian businessmen close to Nicholas upset the Japanese by trading in timber in Korea. On 8 February 1904 the Japanese Navy attacked Dalian and trapped Russia's Pacific fleet.

Source 6

The main areas of conflict with Japan.

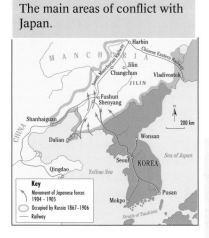

Source 7

A Japanese propaganda leaflet produced for British readers.

Meanwhile, on 20 December 1904, Putilov, the biggest industrial works in St Petersburg, sacked four workers. Father George Gapon called his trade union, the Assembly of Russian Factory and Plant Workers, out on strike in protest. Soon factories all over St Petersburg had to close. By 8 January 1905, 120,000 workers were on strike. There was no electricity.

The Union of Liberation helped Father Gapon write a petition to take to the Tsar at the Winter Palace on Sunday 9 January. The petition asked for pity for the workers on strike, an elected parliament and a constitution.

Bloody Sunday

The night before the march to the Winter Palace, many workers wrote farewell letters to their families and friends in case they were killed. As they marched towards the centre of the city the workers carried religious pictures and sang hymns. At key points soldiers tried to stop them getting too close to the Winter Palace.

Alexandra Kollontai, a revolutionary, marched with the demonstrators and reached the square in front of the Winter Palace. This is what she saw:

Source 8

Alexandra Kollontai, quoted in Barbara Evans Clements, *Bolshevik Feminist*, 1979. Alexandra Kollontai joined the Bolsheviks in 1904 and taught the ideas of Marx to classes of workers. She wrote leaflets calling for the overthrow of Tsar Nicholas.

> I noticed that mounted troops stood drawn up in front of the Winter Palace itself, but everyone thought that it did not mean anything in particular. All the workers were peaceful and expectant. They wanted the Tsar or one of his highest, gold-braided ministers to come before the people and take the humble petition.

The soldiers were frightened. They fired warning shots into the air but the large crowd pushed forward. Unable to stop them, the soldiers began to fire into the unarmed crowd. Alexandra Kollentai remembers what happened next:

Source 9

Quoted in Barbara Evans Clements, *Bolshevik Feminist*, 1979.

> At first I saw the children who were hit [by rifle fire] and dragged down from the trees .... We heard the clatter of hooves. The Cossacks rode right into the crowd and slashed with their sabres like madmen. A terrible confusion arose.

There were more massacres in other parts of the city. Journalists reported that 4,600 people were killed or wounded. The government claimed that 130 were killed and 299 were wounded. Historians now think 200 were killed and 800 were wounded. This is why Sunday 9 January 1905 is known as 'Bloody Sunday'.

Revolution

Bloody Sunday was the start of a year of murders, strikes and protests which forced Tsar Nicholas to promise changes in the government of the Empire. Historians have called these events the Revolution of 1905.

In February terrorists murdered the Tsar's uncle and close friend, Grand Duke Sergei Aleksandrovich. This shook Nicholas badly. He began to listen to friends who advised him to make changes.

In March people heard that the Japanese had killed 89,000 Russian soldiers in a battle for the Manchurian city of Shenyang. Worse, in a spectacular sea battle in the Straits of Tsushima (Source 6) on 27–28 May, the Japanese fleet sank all of Russia's Black Sea fleet of battleships and many of their support ships –

Source 10

A French print made soon after Bloody Sunday.
The priest holding up the cross is Father Gapon.

LES ÉMEUTES DE SAINT-PÉTERSBOURG
La Troupe refoule les Émeutiers conduits par le Pope Gapon

the worst disaster in Russian naval history.

People in professions, like lawyers, doctors, teachers and business-men, now formed unions like the workers. In May all unions joined together in a 'Union of Unions' and set up a central committee to organise it called the St Petersburg Soviet.

In June, in the Black Sea port of Odessa, the crew of the battleship Potemkin mutinied and joined striking workers. Russian troops again opened fire killing an estimated 2,000 people and seriously injuring 3,000 people. Events came to a head in October 1905. On 14 October the Union of Unions brought out all of St Petersburg on strike. Trepov, the governor-general of St Petersburg, could not promise to restore law and order without another massacre. Nicholas was now on the verge of being overthrown from power.

Questions

1   Why did liberals and revolutionaries agree to work together against the Tsar by 1905?

2   Study Source 5. Use the information on page 23 to decide how fair Witte was in blaming Nicholas alone for the war with Japan.

3   In a report on who was to blame for Bloody Sunday, write a sentence on each of the following: Father Gapon, the Union of Liberation, the workers, the soldiers.

4   **a** What effect did Bloody Sunday and news of defeats by Japan have throughout the Empire?
    b Which was the most important cause of revolution?

2.3 How the Tsar survived the 1905 revolution

Reluctantly, the Tsar listened to Witte who now believed that the only way to stop a revolution was to give the liberals – but not the revolutionaries – what they wanted. This would mean an end to autocracy, and an elected Duma with power to make laws. So, on 17 October, Tsar Nicholas signed what was called the October Manifesto. It saved him from the revolution.

The October Manifesto

The October Manifesto promised three things:

- civil liberty (for example, the right to free speech, or the right to hold meetings, etc.);
- a Duma, or parliament, elected by universal suffrage (the right of all adults to vote);
- all laws to be made and approved by the Duma.

There was great rejoicing and celebration. The St Petersburg Soviet voted to end the general strike. Strikes also ended in other cities like Moscow. The Manifesto had a temporary calming effect on the workers in the cities.

But Tsar Nicholas had no intention of keeping any of these promises because he had been forced to make them under pressure. The word 'constitution' was cleverly left out of the Manifesto. The Tsar still called himself an autocrat.

Pogroms and peasant violence
Extreme conservatives loyal to the Tsar reacted violently to the October Manifesto with murders and pogroms. Peasants heard

Source 1

Boris Kustodiev's painting, *The Bolshevik*, 1905, portrays a revolutionary as a heroic giant striding though the streets of Moscow.

that these murders and pogroms were not being punished and started seizing land. They did not attack the landlords themselves but tried to force them to leave their estates; they cut down the landlords' forests, smashed machinery, refused to pay rent, sent their cattle to graze on landlords' fields and set fire to their houses.

Armed uprising fails

In the big cities, revolutionaries were quick to realise that there had not been a revolution at all. Trotsky, who had become chairman of the St Petersburg Soviet, called for an armed rising.

The police quickly arrested the Soviet and put half of its members in prison. Trotsky was sent into exile in Siberia. Meanwhile, in Moscow, the Bolshevik-led Soviet called a strike which paralysed the city. The government sent in troops and a fierce battle took place which destroyed large parts of the old city and killed over 1,000 people. The government crushed the revolution and followed this up with executions of those involved.

The Bolshevik leader, Lenin, did not play a big part in these events. He advised his followers on what weapons to use but when close to danger himself his first instinct was to run. A Bolshevik, Tatiana Aleksinki, remembered how he behaved during one demonstration:

Source 2

This cartoon of 1905 portrays a revolutionary as a gigantic spectre striding through the streets.

Source 3

Tatiana Aleksinki quoted in *La Grande Revue XXVII*, No. 8 Aug 1923

When someone, spotting the cavalry charging the crowd, shouted 'Cossacks', Lenin was the first to flee. He jumped over a barrier. His bowler hat fell off revealing his bare skull perspiring and glittering under the sunlight. He fell, got up, and continued to run ...

Questions

1 How did Count Witte save Tsar Nicholas from the being overthrown?

2 Look at Sources 1 and 2.
  a What similarities and what difference are there in the way each picture portrays revolutionaries?
  b Study Source 1. To what extent does the painting convey a true image of the part played by the Bolsheviks?

3 Look at Source 3. Compare the roles of Trotsky and Lenin in the events of 1905.

2.4 Repression, reform and scandal

Source 1

Peter Arkadevich Stolypin (1862–1911). Stolypin was highly educated and determined to modernise Russia. Within a month of becoming Prime Minister he narrowly escaped a bomb attack on his house by Socialist Revolutionaries. The bomb killed 27 people and injured both his children.

Following the events of 1905, the Tsar became more repressive in the way he ruled Russia. He chose an able, tough man called Peter Stolypin to strengthen his authority and to restore law and order. This section presents two sides of Stolypin: a much-hated man who used ruthless methods; and a reformer who wanted to modernise Russia. It also introduces a character who was to undo much of Stolypin's work, the strange 'holy man', Grigori Rasputin.

Broken promises

The October Manifesto had promised everyone the vote. The Electoral Law for the first elections in Russia's history broke this promise. The system of voting was 'fixed' so that the votes of landowners and property owners were worth more than those of peasants and workers. And while elections were taking place, Fundamental Laws were published which made it clear that the Duma would have fewer powers than the October Manifesto promised:

• The Tsar kept his title of 'autocrat'.
• The Tsar alone made laws.
• The Tsar alone controlled foreign affairs.
• The Duma had no say in military matters.
• The Tsar alone could appoint and dismiss ministers.
• The Tsar could dissolve the Duma (close it down) and use emergency powers to rule the Empire until a new Duma was elected.

The first Duma lasted only 72 days. The Duma voted that it had no confidence in the Tsar's government and demanded that the Tsar form a new government of ministers chosen from the Duma. The Tsar's answer was to dissolve the Duma.

Tsar Nicholas resented Witte for advising him to sign the October Manifesto. Witte soon had difficulty forming a government. Liberals refused to help him, so Witte resigned.

In January 1906 Socialist Revolutionaries launched a new campaign of terror in the countryside to make people lose faith in the government. Between 1906 and 1907 they killed or maimed over 9,000 people. In July 1906 Nicholas chose a new Prime Minister, Peter Stolypin.

Repression

Stolypin used the emergency powers of the Fundamental Laws to set up 'Field Courts for Civilians'. These had the power to deal with anyone whose guilt seemed so obvious that no further investigation was necessary. The accused had to be put on trial within 24 hours of the crime and could not appeal. A death sentence had to be carried out within 24 hours of being found guilty.

Over the next eight months the Field Courts sentenced 1,000 people to death. The nickname for the gallows used to hang the 'guilty' was 'Stolypin's neckties'. To back up the 'Field Courts for

■ Why were the gallows nicknamed 'Stolypin's neckties'?

Civilians' ordinary courts convicted 16,440 people for political crimes and violent attacks in 1908 and 1909. They sentenced 3,682 to death and 4,517 to hard labour.

Why was it so difficult for Stolypin to reform Russia?

However, Stolypin did not believe that crushing terrorism was the answer to Russia's problems. There were two main problems:

1 Russia badly needed to improve methods of farming. More food was needed to feed the growing numbers of workers in new industries. Farm produce could also be sold abroad to pay for urgently needed machinery and raw materials.

2 Since the 1905 revolution the peasants' old loyalty to the Tsar could no longer be relied upon.

Stolypin's solution

Stolypin believed that by making more peasants better off they would remain loyal to the Tsar. He saw that in the western provinces, where single peasant families farmed whole plots of land, they produced more to sell and were better off. However, in central Russia the peasants did not own land as individuals. They farmed scattered strips of land shared out by the village commune or *mir*. They produced barely enough to feed themselves and were not as well off as the peasants in the west who had their own farms.

Stolypin therefore encouraged peasants to leave the communes and become independent farmers. From 5 October 1906 they no longer had to have the permission of the communes to leave. They could borrow money more easily to buy land. The Tsar gave up more of his land for sale, and the government gave help to peasants wanting to set up farms in Siberia and Central Asia.

■ Give two reasons why Stolypin encouraged peasants to leave communes and become independent farmers.

Were Stolypin's reforms a success?

Only 2 per cent of peasants left the communes. The communes gave 75 per cent of those who left the same scattered fields to farm. By 1917 90 per cent of all peasants still farmed land in scattered strips.

The peasants still resented the idea of private ownership of land. They did not think much of Stolypin's reforms. Nevertheless between 1905 and 1914 the number of the gentry class owning land fell by 12.6 per cent. Their land was bought by the peasants.

By 1917 Russia was a country of peasant farmers who owned their own farms either in communes (90 per cent) or as independent families (10 per cent). Together they produced only a third of the crops harvested in much smaller countries like Britain, Belgium and the Netherlands.

■ What changes, if any, did Stolypin make to farming in Russia?

Scandal

While Stolypin crushed revolutionaries and tried to modernise farming methods, he had other worries. There was another obstacle to strengthening the authority of the Tsar – a scandal.

Source 2

Tsar Nicholas II (second from left), and his son Alexis in 1913. Alexis is being carried by a Cossack officer.

The scandal started in 1904 when the Tsarina gave birth to a boy, Alexis. From his mother he inherited a rare blood disease, haemophilia. If he cut himself he sometimes bled for weeks. Knocks caused painful swellings, bruises and internal bleeding. Doctors could do nothing for him.

Then, in 1905, Alexandra found a holy man from Siberia called Rasputin who had special powers to stop bleeding and pain. No one knows how he did this. However, people noticed something unusual about his eyes. They noticed too that Rasputin was a heavy drinker and that he fascinated women. His influence over the Tsarina, Alexandra, made him enemies. Source 3 is a letter said to be written by the Tsarina, and stolen from Rasputin. It gives us an idea of why people grew to dislike him:

Source 3

A letter stolen from Rasputin, 1911. Quoted in Alex de Jonge, *The Life and Times of Grigori Rasputin*, 1982.

My much loved never to be forgotten teacher, saviour and instructor, I am so wretched without you. My soul is only rested and at ease when you, my teacher, are near me. I kiss your hands and lay my head upon your blessed shoulder. I feel so joyful then. Then all I want is sleep, sleep for ever on your shoulder, in your embrace ....

Soon all of St Petersburg was talking about Rasputin. Source 4 shows what people were thinking. Stolypin ordered the Okhrana to have Rasputin watched. But while he was collecting evidence to discredit Rasputin, a police informer who worked for the Okhrana shot Stolypin during an opera performance in September 1911.

Source 4

Cartoon of Rasputin holding the Tsar and Tsarina in his hands.

■ What is the message of this cartoon? Why did people view Rasputin like this?

Questions

1 Stolypin tried to strengthen the Tsar's authority in two ways: repression and reform.
a Give examples of Stolypin's repression.
b Give an example of Stolypin's reforms.
c Why did Stolypin find it difficult to reform Russia?

2 Would Stolypin's reforms have had more success if Rasputin had not caused a scandal at court? Explain your answer.

Review

1 Imagine you have to make a television history programme about the causes of 1905 revolution. You are allowed to use only six scenes. To plan the programme, you have been given the 'story board' below with the titles of each of the six scenes. Describe or make labelled drawings of what you will show in each scene:

1 Life in Russia	2 How Nicholas II ruled his Empire	3 Liberals and revolutionaries
4 Plehve	5 War with Japan	6 Bloody Sunday

2 Lenin viewed the events of 1905 as a 'dress rehearsal' for a revolution rather than an actual revolution. In a dress rehearsal the actors practise and learn from their mistakes. What mistakes did the revolutionaries make and what lessons were there to learn from them?

3 Did Stolypin succeed or fail to strengthen the rule of Tsar Nicholas? Refer in your answer to:

• Repression
• Reform
• Scandal

Unit 3 • War and revolution 1914–1917

Source 1

A Bolshevik anti-war poster. The soldier standing with the whip is probably meant to be German. The person seated on the stretcher is the Tsar. Notice the priest with his arm around the throne.

■ What message about the war did Bolsheviks want to give to those who saw this poster ?

ЦАРЬ, ПОП И БОГАЧ
НА ПЛЕЧАХ У ТРУДОВОГО НАРОДА

Germany declared war on Russia in 1914. Russia was in no state to fight a long war. Within three years there was another revolution. This time Tsar Nicholas did not survive.

3.1 Why did Russia go to war in 1914?

Russia's defeat in the war of 1904–1905 nearly forced Nicholas to give up being Tsar. Why then did he take Russia to war again in 1914? Source 2 suggests more than one reason why Russia was likely to go to war in 1914. Study boxes 1–5, in that order, to find out what they were. But which was the most important? This section outlines three interpretations of why Russia went to war. Which do you find the most convincing?

Source 2

Reasons why Russia and its neighbours were likely to go to war in 1914.

3 Russia and France have an agreement (1894) to help each other if attacked by Germany. In 1912 France agrees to help modernise Russia'army so that Russia can mobilise for war faster

RUSSIAN EMPIRE

Russia's Black Sea fleet has to go through the Dardanelles to get to the Mediterranean Sea. Whoever controls the Balkans can stop the Russian fleet from passing through

2 Germany's Schlieffen Plan (1905) is to crush France quickly

GERMANY
before Russia has time to mobilise its army, then to conquer Russia

1 Austria's ambition to expand north is blocked by Germany, who encourages Austria to expand south

FRANCE

AUSTRIA-HUNGARY
Serbia, however, stands in the way

ITALY

Sarajevo

ROMANIA

SERBIA

BULGARIA

Black Sea

Dardanelles

ALBANIA   GREECE

TURKEY
4 The Muslim Turkish Empire is breaking up. Russia wins influence in the Balkans by backing Christians who want to break free from Turkish rule

THE BALKAN STATES
5 The Balkan peoples break free from rule by Turkey in a series of rebellions and wars. They want to stay independent and to increase their size

Mediterranean Sea

Interpretation 1: Russia wanted to stay a great power

The war began when Austria-Hungary declared war on Serbia on 28 June 1914. Serbia is at the centre of the Balkan region. Whichever country controlled the region could also take control of the Turkish Straits (Source 2). It would then be able to stop Russian warships getting from the Black Sea to the Mediterranean Sea. Having a powerful navy was one of the things that made Russia a great power.

To stay a great power, Russia therefore had to help Serbia stand up to Austria-Hungary and its ally Germany (the Central Powers). As one historian put it:

Source 3

F.R. Bridge, *1914, The Coming of the First World War*, 1983.

If the Central Powers were allowed to destroy Serbia they would control not only the Balkans but the Straits – the sea passage from the Black Sea to the Mediterranean Sea. Russia would be reduced from a Great Power .... This was what was at stake for the Tsarist Government.

Interpretation 2: War plans and railway timetables started it

In 1894 France and Russia agreed to help each other if attacked by Germany. Germany now knew that if she attacked either France or Russia she would have to fight a war on two fronts: France in the West and Russia in the East (Source 2).

In 1895-1905 General von Schlieffen drew up a German war plan to knock out France before Russia was fully ready for war. In those days, the fastest way to mobilise an army (get it ready for war) was by railway. Schlieffen calculated it would take Russia up to 110 days to mobilise; it would take Germany and Austria-Hungary 15 days.

In 1912, however, the French agreed to pay for improvements to Russia's transport system to make Russian mobilisation faster. These improvements would take five years. By 1917 Russia would be able to get ready for war in 18 days. This gave the Germans a motive to look for an excuse to go to war well before 1917.

However, when Tsar Nicholas ordered the Russian army to get ready to defend Serbia, he did not want to go to war. He mobilised the army to threaten Austria-Hungary to leave Serbia alone. But this also meant massing Russian troops along the frontier with Austria-Hungary's ally, Germany. Germany could not risk allowing Russia to mobilise its army first:

Source 4

A.J.P. Taylor, *The First World War*, 1963.

... the Russian decision to mobilise threw out the German timetable. If the Germans did nothing, they would lose the advantage of superior speed. They would have to face war on two fronts, not one; and this they imagined, they could not win .... Germany sent an ultimatum, demanding Russian demobilisation within twelve hours. The Russians refused. On 1 August Germany declared war on Russia; two days later ... on France. The First World War had begun – imposed on the statesmen of Europe by railway timetables.

Interpretation 3: It was the 'financiers' who started it

The Bolsheviks believed Germany wanted to smash the Russian Empire, make the peoples of the Empire slaves, and take over their farmlands, coal, iron and gold mines and their oil fields .

Lenin believed that powerful, greedy men who made their money from the profits of trade and investments (financiers) started the war. They wanted to become richer by conquering more lands. In each country their Church leaders told them that God was on their side. Lenin wrote that it was:

Source 5

Lenin. *Imperialism, the Highest Stage of Capitalism* 1916.

... a war to decide whether the British or German group of financial plunderers* is to receive most riches.
* Plunderers: those who take by force.

Questions

1 Decide which, if any, of interpretations 1–3 you find most convincing. Give each a mark out of ten and add a comment to explain your marks.

2 Why is it unlikely that historians will ever agree about why Russia went to war?

3.2 Defeats and victories

Russia had the largest army in the world – 5 million men including reserves. This was bigger than the armies of Germany and Austria-Hungary put together. But soon after the war began, Russia lost one battle after another. Why did this happen when Russia's forces were so much larger than those of its enemies?

Why did the Russian armies do so badly in the war?

The war started well for Russia but the generals were careless. The plan was to attack East Prussia with two armies and to attack Austria with four in Galicia (see Source 1).

Source 1

The Eastern Front.

Source 2

Russian prisoners of war after the Battle of Tannenberg.

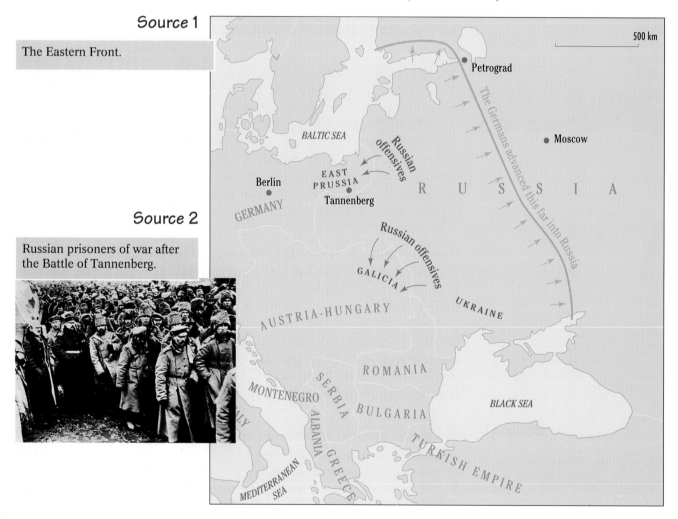

The generals who led the Russian armies behaved as if it were a race to get to Berlin first. They did not work as a team. Their front lines moved so fast that they went too far ahead of their support and supplies. Instead of setting up telephone wires, they sent wireless messages to each other which gave away their positions to the Germans.

In the Battle of Tannenberg (29 August 1914) a German army

killed or put out of action 130,000 Russian soldiers and captured over 100,000 Russian prisoners of war (Source 2). They pushed the Russians out of East Prussia.

Meanwhile, the Russians had more success in the south against Austria-Hungary. They broke through the enemy front in Galicia and sent the Austrians into retreat. They captured 100,000 prisoners of war and 400 artillery guns, knocking out a third of the Austro-Hungarian army.

The Russian army was not well led. The Minister of War, General Sukhomlinov, did not think much of modern methods of war. He and his generals' favourite weapon was the bayonet. Their preferred method of attack was to storm enemy positions and destroy them in hand-to-hand combat. Against the machine guns and barbed wire of the well-equipped German army, such attacks were suicidal. In one battle fought in Poland:

Source 3

J. Buchan, *A History of the Great War*, 1920.

Men were flung into the firing line without rifles, armed only with a sword-bayonet in one hand and a bomb in the other. That meant fighting, desperate fighting, at the closest of quarters.

By February 1915 about half of the soldiers who arrived to fight in the front-line trenches had to wait to pick up rifles from those who were killed. Just as bad was the shortage of 76mm shells for the field artillery. The government factories could produce only 9,000 shells a month.

News of high casualties caused alarm in different parts of the Empire. In Baku, the capital of Azerbaijan, women lay on the rails to stop troop trains moving. In Kazakhstan there was violent resistance to conscription (compulsory military service).

Russia's allies tried to send help, but the Germans and Austro-Hungarians blocked off Russia's trade routes in the west. So supplies had to be sent to ports like Murmansk and Archangel in the north (see page 56). In 1914 there was no railway line to Murmansk. The port of Archangel was frozen six months of the year and was linked to the rest of Russia by a single track railway. Supplies from Britain and France just piled up on the dockside.

The Germans launched a fierce attack in April 1915. By July they had forced the Russians to retreat from Poland. The Austrians forced a similar retreat in Galicia. Together Germany and Austria-Hungary soon took control of 13 per cent of the Russian Empire's population – over 16 million people (Source 1).

Questions

1 How does Source 3 help explain Germany's success against the Russian armies up to 1915?

2 For what other reasons did the Russian armies do so badly against Germany?

3 What signs were there that the war could cause the Russian peoples to try to break free from the Empire?

3.3 Nicholas, Alexandra, Rasputin and the war

Civilians at first blamed the disasters of the war on the Tsar's ministers, not on Nicholas. Nicholas wisely decided to allow civilians rather than the army to run the factories producing shells, rifles and equipment for the war. The results were excellent. By February 1917 there were no shortages of ammunition and weapons. With the help of British soldiers, a railway line was built from Murmansk and the railway to Archangel was improved.

Source 1

A Russian painting of 1917 shows Tsar Nicholas holding up an icon, or holy picture, as he blesses soldiers in the Russian army. It is based on a black and white photograph taken in 1915.

Nevertheless, civilians demanded that a new government of ministers be chosen from the Duma. Tsar Nicholas would not listen. Instead he made two foolish mistakes which led to his downfall. First, he sacked his uncle, the Grand Duke Nikolai Nikolaevich, as the Commander-in-Chief of the army and took over command himself. Then he left the Tsarina, Alexandra, in charge of the government.

Why was Nicholas's decision to take personal command of the armed forces such a bad mistake?

While he was at the front leading his armies, Nicholas received a constant stream of advice from Alexandra. Here are some of the things she wrote:

Remember to keep the image [icon] in your hand again and several times to comb your hair with His comb before meeting the ministers. [The comb was a present from Rasputin.]

Be more autocratic my very, very sweetheart, and show your mind.

Sources 2 and 3

Letters of the Tsarina to the Tsar, 1914–16, edited by B. Pares, 1923.

But soon Rasputin was adding his advice on how to run the war:

Now before I forget I must give you a message from our Friend prompted by what he saw in the night. He begs you to order that one should advance near Riga, says it is necessary, otherwise the Germans will settle down so firmly through the winter that it will cost endless bloodshed ....

When Rasputin advised Alexandra to make a former Deputy President of the Duma, Protopopov, Minister of the Interior, Nicholas was not sure this was a good idea:

Source 4

Letters of the Tsarina to the Tsar, 1914–16, edited by B. Pares, 1923, and letters from Nicholas , kept in the Krasnyiarkiv (Red Archive) in Moscow. The affectionate words they use to each other are difficult to translate exactly from the Russian!

[Nicholas:] I must consider this question as it has taken me by surprise. Our Friend's opinions of people are sometimes very strange, as you yourself know – therefore one must be careful, especially with appointments to high places.
[Alexandra:] ... all my trust is in our Friend who only thinks of you, Baby and Russia. And guided by him we shall get through this heavy time .... Sweety mine, you must back me up, for your Baby's sake.
[Nicholas:] Tender thanks for the severe written scolding. Your poor little weak-willed hubby.

Source 5

Rasputin surrounded by admirers at tea. Notice that all except the servant (with the tray holding the glass) are women. His many affairs with such women turned their husbands and relatives into enemies.

Rasputin's behaviour shocked and enraged people. Source 5 is a photograph used by his enemies to get him into trouble. A report by the secret police early in 1916 said:

Source 6

A secret police (Okhrana) report quoted in Alex de Jonge, *The Life and Times of Grigori Rasputin*, 1982.

> ... the filthy gossip about the Tsar's family has now become the property of the street. We must also note together with this feeling of extreme disrespect for the person of Her Majesty the Empress Alexandra Fedorovana the widespread feeling against her as a 'German'. Her Majesty is regarded, even in intellectual circles, as the inspirer and leader of the campaign for a separate peace with Germany.

Unable to bear what was happening any longer, a group of patriotic conservatives decided to murder Rasputin. Their leader, Prince Felix Yusopov, was a close friend of the Tsar's favourite nephew. He told a member of the Duma:

Source 7

Vasilii Maklakov, a Duma Deputy, quoted in R. Pipes, *The Russian Revolution 1899–1919*, 1990. Vasilii Maklakov was a member of the conservative Kadet Party. He criticised Rasputin. Prince Yusopov tried to persuade him to help murder Rasputin.

> Her [the Tsarina's] spiritual balance depends entirely on Rasputin: the instant he is gone, it will disintegrate. And once the Emperor has been freed of Rasputin's and his wife's influence, everything will change; he will turn into a good constitutional monarch.

In December, Yusopov invited Rasputin to his home. There Yusopov fed Rasputin with cakes and wine poisoned with enough potassium cyanide to kill him several times over. When this did not work, Yusopov shot Rasputin in the back. For a moment he thought this had done the trick but Rasputin opened his eyes, leapt up at him and tried to escape. Yusopov's friend, Purishevich, shot him again and kicked Rasputin in the head. His body was then dumped in the River Neva.

Questions

1 Do Sources 1–3 prove it was a mistake for Nicholas to leave Alexandra to run the country in 1915 while he took over command of the army? Divide the reasons in your answer into those which you think prove it was a mistake and those which you think do not.

2 What evidence is there that Rasputin influenced important decisions?

3 Study Source 7. What did Prince Felix Yusopov believe he would achieve by murdering Rasputin?

3.4   The revolution of February 1917

Nicholas narrowly escaped being overthrown in 1905. Disturbances and protests continued to trouble his Empire. But it was not until February 1917 that Nicholas was forced to give up his throne. Why did a revolution finally take place in 1917 but not before? This section investigates the immediate causes of this revolution.

What triggered the revolution?

Cold weather

Was there a link between the weather and the revolution? The average winter temperature of Petrograd (formerly St Petersburg) between January and March 1917 was −12.1° C compared with −4.4° C the year before. To defend Petrograd and protect the Tsarina, 340,000 soldiers were stationed in overcrowded barracks in and around the city. These soldiers were the newest recruits – mostly peasants in uniform. Most of their officers were either newly trained and inexperienced or unable to serve at the front because of war injuries. The soldiers were not the best disciplined in the Russian army. They were cold and often hungry.

Fuel and food shortages

Piles of snow and ice stopped the railways carrying fuel and supplies into the city. Early in 1917 the secret police reported:

Source 1

A secret police report, 1917, quoted in M. Ferro, *Nicholas II, The Last of the Tsars*, 1990.

... the workers here are on the verge of despair. It is thought that the slightest explosion ... will result in uncontrollable riots. The cost of living has trebled, the impossibility of finding food, the loss of time through queuing for hours outside shops ... have become unbearable.

Source 2

Women demonstrating on International Women's Day 23 February 1917.

Women factory workers went on strike. Their menfolk followed. Then fuel shortages caused more factories to stop working. Worse, the bakeries closed. The city's military commander, General Khabalov, decided to introduce rationing. Tempers flared as people who had queued for hours in the biting cold were told that bread had sold out.

Then on 22 February the temperature rose to 8° C. The next day, 23 February, was International Women's Day. Thousands of women took to the streets to demonstrate (Source 2). Soon the men had joined them. Large numbers of people continued to demonstrate and began to turn aggressive. Some of their banners said, 'Down with the German Woman'. Alexandra wrote:

Source 3

Red Archives, 1923, quoted in R. Pipes, *The Russian Revolution*, 1990.

This is a hooligan movement, young people run and shout that there is no bread simply to create excitement, along with workers who prevent others from working. If the weather were very cold they would probably all stay at home. But this will all pass and become calm if only the Duma will behave itself.

The situation began to get out of hand. Nicholas gave General Khabalov the following order:

Source 4

P.E. Shcheglovitiv (ed.), *The Downfall of the Tsarist Regime* 1924–27.

I order you to stop tomorrow the disorders in the capital which are unacceptable.

Mutiny

Bridges across the River Neva were closed to prevent demonstrators massing too close to the city centre. People began to walk across the river because the water was still frozen despite the warmer weather. Officers ordered troops to open fire. The soldiers shot about 40 people before refusing to continue to obey orders. The Duma Deputy, Rodzianko, remembered what happened next:

Source 5

Rodzianko to Ruzskii, quoted in R. Pipes, *The Russian Revolution 1899–1919*, 1990.

Unexpectedly for all, there erupted a soldier mutiny such as I have never seen. These were not soldiers of course but *muzhiks* [peasants] taken directly from the plough who have found it useful now to make known their *muzhik* demands. In the crowd, all one could hear was 'Land and Freedom', 'Down with the Dynasty', 'Down with the Romanovs', 'Down with the Officers'.

Rodzianko sent an urgent telegraph message to the Tsar:

Source 6

Translated from *Revolution in 1917: A Soviet Chronicle*, N. Avdeev et al, 1923–27.

Situation serious .... It is essential at once to entrust a person enjoying country's confidence with the formation of new government.

Meanwhile, twelve Duma Deputies had formed a Provisional Committee to take over the government. The workers, soldiers and sailors of Petrograd formed a Soviet (council) to watch over them.

The Tsar abdicates

The Tsar eventually realised what was happening. He set off from the military headquarters at Mogilev in his royal train for his family home, Tsarskoe Selo. The train stopped at Pskov station. There he learned that his generals would no longer support him. Nicholas decided that Russia stood a better chance of winning the war if he stepped down from his position as Tsar. However, when he learned that if his son became Tsar he would not be allowed to live with him, he decided to abdicate in favour of his brother, Michael. Michael refused to be Tsar. The Russian Empire was without an emperor.

Questions

Study this list of factors which helped to cause the February revolution:

- The women's demonstration in Petrograd on 23 February
- Twelve Duma Deputies formed a Provisional Committee
- The Tsar's son was a haemophiliac
- Alexandra was a German
- The Russian generals refused to help Tsar Nicholas
- The cold weather
- Rasputin
- The rationing of bread
- The mutiny of the soldiers of the Petrograd garrison
- The war
- The workers, soldiers and sailors formed a Soviet
- Nicholas's brother, Michael, refused to become Tsar

1 Decide which of these factors you would put under the separate headings of 'long term' and 'short term' causes.

2 Rank and number the factors under each heading in their order of importance.

3 If the first factor you have chosen for each heading had not existed, could the revolution have happened? Explain your answer.

3.5 Two centres of power

The February revolution left two centres of power – the Provisional Government and the Petrograd Soviet – instead of one strong government. This created the conditions for attempts to seize power by both the Bolsheviks and an army general. The last part of this unit explains why there were two centres of power and why both attempts to seize power failed.

Why was the Provisional Government so weak?

The Petrograd Soviet

The Provisional Committee of Duma Deputies took over the government, but soon the Petrograd Soviet made sure that it could not act without its support. The Soviet gave this order to the armed forces:

Source 1

From Vernadsky, *Source Book of Russian History*, vol. 3.

Order No. 1

In all political actions, troop units must obey the Soviet of Workers' and Soldiers' Deputies ....

The orders of the Military Commission of the State Duma are to be obeyed, with the exception of those instances in which they contradict the orders and decrees of the Soviet of Workers' and Soldiers' Deputies.

The Provisional Government and Petrograd Soviet agreed to hold a general election in November 1917 for a new parliament called the Constituent Assembly. Meanwhile, Russia continued to fight with her allies to defeat Germany and Austria-Hungary. The Soviet wanted the Provisional Government to end the war.

Revolutionaries like Trotsky and Lenin who were out of the country when the February revolution happened began to return to Russia. Joseph Stalin and Kamenev were among the first Bolshevik leaders to reach Petrograd from exile in Siberia after the revolution. Stalin edited the Bolshevik newspaper, *Pravda*. He also helped run the Party until Lenin arrived.

The arrival of Lenin

For some time the Austrians and Germans had supplied the Bolsheviks secretly with money because the Bolsheviks wanted to take Russia out of the war. In April the Germans provided Lenin with a train to return to Russia from Switzerland.

However, when Lenin was given a chance to speak in the Petrograd Soviet, some, including his wife, Nadezhda Krupskaya, feared he was horribly out of touch with how people felt. In a speech lasting 90 minutes Lenin called for the revolution to be finished. This meant he wanted to overthrow the Provisional Government. An eyewitness who was standing close by heard Krupskaya say:

Source 2

Memoirs of George Denicke. His close friend, Pinkevich, was the eyewitness who overheard Krupskaya.

It seems that Ilyich is out of his mind.

Lenin was heckled. A Menshevik called Bogdanov, shouted:

It is obscene to applaud such rubbish. These are the ravings of a lunatic.

Source 3

From C. Porter, *Alexandra Kollontai: A Biography*, 1980.

The only Bolshevik to get to her feet to support Lenin was Alexandra Kollontai.

In another meeting Lenin explained what came to be called his April Theses. These ideas were:

• end the war;
• give all power to the Soviets;
• all property and land to belong to the people;
• world revolution.

Lenin's ideas were cleverly simplified in the slogan: 'Peace, Bread, Land'. This was easy to remember and became more popular as the war continued.

The Bolshevik newspaper *Pravda* at first pretended it had a mechanical breakdown to avoid printing his April Theses. Nevertheless, Lenin soon regained control of his party because no one could match the brilliance of his arguments. Zinoviev and Stalin took second and third position behind him. They set up a Military Organisation to seize power.

The June Offensive

In May a number of socialists from the Soviet joined the Provisional Government. The Socialist Revolutionary, Kerensky, became War Minister. He whipped up enthusiasm for continuing the war:

Source 4

E.H.Wilcox, *Russia's Ruin*, 1919.

Crowds gathered for hours to catch a glimpse of him. His path was everywhere strewn with flowers. Soldiers ran for miles after his motor car, trying to shake his hand or kiss the hem of his garment.

Kerensky inspired the country to support the Army in a fresh attack on the Austrians. However, this attack, known as the 'June Offensive', was a failure. In the cities bread rations were reduced even more. Rail workers went on strike. More serious still, the workers from the Putilov arms factory went on strike. Trouble once again boiled over on to the streets of Petrograd and in other cities like Moscow. Stalin organised a demonstration of soldiers and workers against the war.

Trotsky soon overshadowed Stalin and the other senior Bolsheviks. Lenin persuaded him to join the Bolsheviks. Together they turned people's anger with the war and criticism of the

Source 5

Kerensky visiting the front in 1917.

government to the Bolsheviks' advantage. The Bolsheviks began to arm the factory workers and formed them into Red Guard units.

On 20 June an entire machine gun regiment mutinied and 20,000 sailors arrived in Petrograd, demanding that the Bolsheviks take over the government. But just then the Provisional Government released information about how Lenin was receiving help from the Germans. Lenin quickly went into hiding and escaped to Finland. Other Bolshevik leaders, including Trotsky and Kollontai, were caught and put in prison.

The Kornilov affair

On 11 July Kerensky became Prime Minister and appointed a popular new Commander-in-Chief of the Army – General Kornilov (Source 6).

Kerensky wanted to stay in power after the general elections to the new Constituent Assembly (parliament) in November 1917. To stay popular he had to get on well with the Petrograd Soviet. But the Soviet made it difficult for army leaders like Kornilov to win the war. Order No. 1 (see Source 1) meant it was hard for officers to keep discipline and for the army to make quick decisions. Kerensky feared that the army generals might make a move against his government; he thought they were a bigger threat to the Provisional Government than the Bolsheviks.

It seems that Kerensky was right. In August Kornilov mutinied and tried to seize power. Kerensky panicked. To defend Petrograd from Kornilov he released the Bolsheviks from prison and armed them. But Kornilov's soldiers deserted him before he could get to Petrograd. He was arrested.

The army now hated Kerensky. Even civilians no longer trusted him. This opened the way for the Bolsheviks to seize power. In

Source 6

Kornilov being carried by soldiers on his arrival in Moscow, 14 August 1917.

September 1917, while Lenin spent much of his time in hiding, the workers again chose Trotsky to be Chairman of the Petrograd Soviet. He was a much better speaker than Lenin. This is how a Menshevik eyewitness described one of his speeches:

Source 7

N. Sukhanov, *Notes on the Revolution*, 1923. Sukhanov supported the Mensheviks and took an active part in the events of 1917.

The mood of the audience of over three thousand, filling the hall, was definitely one of excitement; their hush indicated expectation .... Trotsky at once began to heat up the atmosphere with skill and brilliance .... Trotsky knew what he was doing .... Soviet power [Trotsky said] was destined not only to put an end to the suffering in the trenches. It would provide land and end internal disorder .... The mood around me verged on ecstasy. It seemed that the mob would at any moment, spontaneously and unasked, burst into some kind of religious hymn .... I watched this truly grandiose spectacle with an unusually heavy heart.

Questions

1 Read Source 1. In what ways would this Order have helped or hindered the work of the Provisional Government?

2 Read Sources 2 and 3. For what reasons do you think Krupskaya and Bogdanov reacted in the way they did to Lenin's speech?

3 Study Sources 4 and 5.
   a What do they suggest about soldiers' attitudes towards Kerensky in the summer of 1917?
   b How do you explain this attitude?

4 Why do you think the author of Source 7 watched with 'an unusually heavy heart'?

5 For what different reasons did the Bolsheviks and Kornilov fail to seize power between July and August 1917?

Review

Timeline: a summary of the main events, 1914–1917

1914 Aug	Germany declared war on Russia.
1915 Aug	Tsar Nicholas took command of the armed forces. He left the Tsarina to run the government.
1916 Dec	A small group of patriotic conservatives murdered Rasputin.
1917 Feb 23	International Women's Day. Thousands of women in Petrograd led demonstrations of hungry workers.
Feb 26/7 28	The Petrograd garrison of soldiers mutinied. Twelve members of the Duma formed the Provisional Committee. Soldiers, sailors and workers formed the Petrograd Soviet.
Mar 2	The Tsar agreed to abdicate.
April	The Germans helped Lenin and other revolutionaries return to Russia.
June	The Russian army launched a fresh attack on Austria which failed.
July	The Provisional Government arrested Bolshevik leaders for plotting to overthrow it. Lenin escaped.
July 11	Kerensky became Prime Minister and made General Kornilov Commander-in-Chief of the army.
Aug 27	Kornilov tried to seize power; Kerensky released the Bolsheviks from prison to help defend the government.

The dates up to February 1917 are those of the old Russian calendar which was twelve days behind the western calendar.

Use the timeline above and the information in Unit 3 to help you answer these questions:

1 **a** Which of the following affected the situation in Russia before the revolution in 1917 as well as the situation before the revolution of 1905 (see Unit 2): war, food shortages, strikes, existence of a Duma, army support for the Tsar, the Tsarina's control of the government?
  b In what ways were the two situations different?

2 **a** In what ways were the war, the weather, the Tsarina and Rasputin to blame for Nicholas's downfall?
  b To what extent was Tsar Nicholas to blame for his own downfall?

3 Why did the February revolution leave two centres of power?

4 What effect did the failure of the June Offensive and the Kornilov affair have on Kerensky's Provisional Government?

Unit 4 • The Empire changes hands

Lenin from Sergei Eisenstein's film October.

4.1 The Bolsheviks seize power

In a coup d'etat* on 25/26 October 1917, Lenin's Bolshevik Party suddenly and easily got rid of Kerensky's Provisional Government. How was this possible when only one out of 600 Russians supported the Bolsheviks? The first section of this unit asks you to consider four possible reasons for this. Did the Bolsheviks succeed because they were well prepared, or because the Provisional Government did too little to stop them? Was it the leadership of Lenin and Trotsky or the disunity of their opponents which gave them victory?

coup d'etat, or coup
A sudden, often violent, overthrow of a government carried out by a small group.

How did the Bolsheviks take power with so little support?

How well prepared were the Bolsheviks?
Lenin's clear ideas guided the planning and tactics of the Bolshevik Party. The Provisional Government knew all along what the Bolsheviks were up to. However, they did too little too late to stop them. Examine the following sequence of events in 1917.

In August 1917 the mutiny of General Kornilov panicked the Provisional Government. It released the Bolsheviks from prison and gave them weapons to help defend Petrograd against General Kornilov. Throughout September the Bolsheviks worked hard to win the support of most workers in the Petrograd and Moscow Soviets. The Bolsheviks put pressure on the leaders of the Petrograd Soviet to call a Second Congress (meeting) of all the Soviets on 25 October.

The German advance towards Petrograd strengthened the hand of the Bolsheviks who agreed to let the Petrograd Soviet use their military organisation to help defend the city. On 10 October the Bolshevik leaders secretly decided to use this defence force to seize power just before the second Congress of all the Soviets met on 25 October.

Did the Provisional Government do enough to prevent a coup?
On 24 October Kerensky ordered the army to get ready to prevent a possible Bolshevik attempt to seize power. Were the precautions they took enough? Look carefully at the map of Petrograd (Source 1), then examine the sequence of events which follows and judge for yourself.

Source 1

Petrograd in 1917.

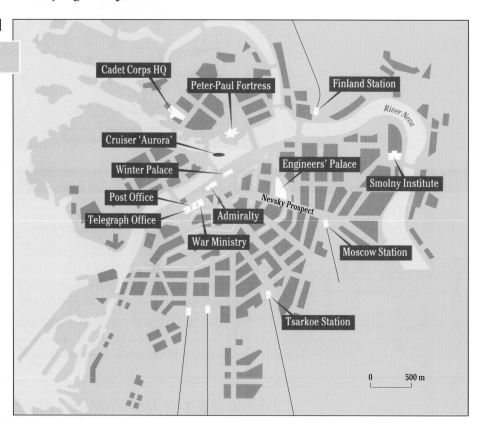

- They cut the telephone wires to the Bolsheviks' headquarters in the Smolni Institute (once a college for girls).
- They raised the bridges over the River Neva to stop crowds entering the city centre.
- They sent the following to guard and protect the Provisional Government in the Winter Palace:

– three detachments of student soldiers (cadets);
– the women's death battalion (140 volunteers);
– a bicycle unit;
– 40 war invalids led by an officer with an artificial leg;
– some light artillery (guns which fired shells).

The army sent no machine guns to defend the Winter Palace and left their own headquarters (the Engineers' Palace) unguarded.

Who led the Bolshevik coup and how was it done?

Trotsky, not Lenin, planned and organised how the Bolsheviks seized power. The coup started on the night of 24 October before the Second Congress of Soviets met. It was Trotsky's idea to use the Congress as a cover to seize power and to claim it was all done for the Soviet.

On 24 October the Bolsheviks used the cover of darkness to take control, one by one, of railway stations, post offices, telephone centres, banks, bridges, and the Engineers' Palace (the military headquarters). There was little resistance; no shots were fired.

While this was happening, Lenin arrived at the Bolshevik headquarters heavily disguised and wearing a wig and glasses. As soon as a few people passing saw through his disguise he hid. Trotsky came and went to keep him up to date with the latest news. In between these times Lenin tried to catch some sleep on the floor. At 10 a.m. the next day he released this statement to the press:

Source 2

The Bolsheviks' First Decree, 25 October 1917.

> TO THE CITIZENS OF RUSSIA! The Provisional Government has been deposed. Government authority has passed into the hands of the organ of the Petrograd Soviet of Workers' and Soldiers' Deputies, the Military Revolutionary Committee ....

The leaders of the Petrograd Soviet did not want the Congress to support what the Bolsheviks had done. Angrily they put out this statement:

Source 3

N. Avdeev, *A Soviet History of the 1917 Revolution*, 1923–1930.

> The Central Executive Committee considers the Second Congress as not having taken place and regards it as a private gathering of Bolshevik delegates.

That afternoon, the leader of the Provisional Government, Kerensky, borrowed a car from the American Embassy and went to look for loyal soldiers. The remaining members of the government stayed in the Winter Palace, waiting for him to return with help.

Kerensky did not return. At 6.30 p.m. the Bolsheviks ordered the Provisional Government to surrender or be shot at from the guns of the battle cruiser, Aurora, and the Peter Paul Fortress (on the other side of the river). At 9.00 p.m. the Aurora fired a few blank shots which failed to scare the Provisional Government who stayed in the Winter Palace. Then at 11.00 p.m. the guns of the Peter Paul Fortress opened fire but this too caused only slight damage to the Winter Palace.

Source 4

A scene from Sergei Eisenstein's film, *October*, which shows Bolsheviks storming the Winter Palace which had become the headquarters of the Provisional Government. Eisenstein made the film in 1927 – three years after Lenin had died. No single leader had yet taken Lenin's place. To prevent Trotsky from becoming leader, Stalin and other senior Bolsheviks ganged up against him. Before the public could see the film, they made Eisenstein cut out the scenes showing Trotsky's part in the coup.

Only the Women's Death Battalion and a few teenage cadets were brave enough to stay to defend the Provisional Government. They tried to come out to fight but were quickly surrounded and forced to surrender. At this point Bolshevik Red Guards and sailors sneaked in through the unlocked gates and open windows of the Winter Palace. At 2.10 a.m. they arrested the Provisional Government.

Only five people were killed during these events – mostly shot by stray bullets. Mobs only entered, looted and vandalised the Winter Palace after it ceased defending itself. But this was not how the Bolsheviks later wanted their coup to be remembered. Source 4, a still from Sergei Eisenstein's pro-Bolshevik film *October*, shows the official Bolshevik version of these events.

Questions

1 a How did the Bolsheviks prepare to seize power?
  b Which other events helped the Bolsheviks to seize power?

2 What more could the Provisional Government have done to prevent the Bolshevik coup?

3 Look at Source 4.
  a What does the film-maker want the viewer to believe about this event?
  b What facts show that Source 4 gives a false image of what really happened?
  c Why do you think the Bolsheviks wanted to portray the events of 25 October in this way? Explain your answer.
  d Suggest possible reasons why, ten years later, Trotsky's rivals wanted his part in the coup cut from the film.

4.2 Dictatorship

Lenin wasted very little time before setting up a dictatorship. Within days he and the Bolsheviks had taken over all branches of the government. How were they able to do this when they had so little support?

Why was Lenin able to create a dictatorship?

As soon as the Second Congress opened at 10.40 p.m. on 24 October, the Socialist Revolutionaries and Mensheviks made it clear what they thought of the Bolshevik takeover. The Mensheviks said that the

Source 1

K.G. Kotelnikov, Second Congress of all Russian Soviets, 1928.

...military conspiracy was organised and carried out by the Bolshevik Party in the name of the Soviets behind the backs of all the other parties and groups represented in the Soviets ....

The Mensheviks and the more moderate Socialist Revolutionaries then walked out. Trotsky replied:

Source 2

N. Sukhanov, *Notes on the Revolution*, Vol. 7, 1922–1923.

Go where you belong, to the dustbin of history.

Those left behind were Bolshevik supporters who included some Socialist Revolutionaries (the Left Socialist Revolutionaries). Together they approved of what the Bolshevik leaders did next.

Lenin set up a new temporary government called the Council of People's Commissars (Sovnarkom). He chose the members of this government. Nearly all were Bolsheviks; a few were Left Socialist Revolutionaries. Lenin made himself Prime Minister. He fined anyone who was late to meetings (five roubles for less than half an hour; ten roubles for more) and no one was allowed to speak for too long. When there was discussion, it was typical for Lenin to read a book and only join in to give his decision.

The Second Congress agreed to replace the group that led the Petrograd Soviet with a new Central Executive Committee (Ispolkom). Until the general election on 12 November this would act like a temporary parliament to keep an eye on the Council of People's Commissars. However, the Bolshevik leaders handpicked the members of Ispolkom. All the real decisions were taken outside Sovnarkom and Ispolkom by Lenin and the leaders of the Bolshevik Party.

From the start Lenin ruled by decrees. These were orders which had the force of law. The first was a decree on peace. It said that negotiations for an end to the war would start immediately. The second was a decree on land. All government and church lands, and properties of landlords not used for farming, were to be transferred to the peasant communes for their use.

Most of the soldiers in the Russian Army were peasants eager to grab their share of the land. They deserted in large numbers while the German armies and their allies continued to advance into Russia.

Other decrees which followed gave the impression that the Bolsheviks were in control. A decree on the press banned all non-Bolshevik newspapers. A decree on work promised workers an 8-hour day and a 48-hour week with strict rules about holidays and overtime.

On 7 December Lenin set up a secret police force called the 'Cheka' or the 'All-Russian Extraordinary Commission to fight Counter-Revolution and Espionage'. It was Lenin's version of the Tsar's Okhrana.

After the February revolution, most people were looking forward to Russia's first, democratic, general election for a new Constituent Assembly (parliament) on 12 November. The results of the election (Source 3) did not surprise Lenin. He delayed the opening of the Constituent Assembly until 5 January 1918. When it did open, Lenin sent in Bolshevik troops to close it down.

Source 3

R. Pipes, *The Russian Revolution 1899–1919*, 1990.

General election results	
Socialist Revolutionaries	40.4%
Bolsheviks	24.0%
Mensheviks	2.6%
Left Socialist Revolutionaries	1.0%
Other socialist parties	0.9%
Constitutional-Democrats (Kadets)	4.7%
Other liberal and non-socialist parties	2.8%
National minority parties (Examples: Ukrainian SR's and Georgian Mensheviks)	13.4%
Results not known	10.2%

Questions

1 The Mensheviks and the moderate Socialist Revolutionaries walked out of the Congress of Soviets on 24 October. How did this help Lenin?

2 Power was meant to be shared by two bodies, Sovnarkom and Ispolkom. Why did Ispolkom actually have very little power?

3 In what ways did the Bolshevik decrees on peace and land help strengthen their control?

4 Look at Source 3. Why do you think Lenin ignored the election results and closed down the Constituent Assembly?

4.3 Peace, civil war, and terror

To cling on to power, the Bolsheviks paid a heavy price for peace with Germany, fought a civil war and used terror against those who did not support them. By 1921 they had won the civil war, eliminated their enemies, and strengthened their dictatorship. This section looks at the roles played by several Bolsheviks in these events, and asks which of them was chiefly responsible for the Bolshevik victory.

Why did the Bolsheviks win the civil war?

The Treaty of Brest-Litovsk
Trotsky represented Russia in peace talks with Germany to end the war. Despite his efforts the Germans demanded a heavy price. As Source 1 shows, Russia lost all its western lands, 26 per cent of its population, 27 per cent of its farmland, 2 per cent of its

Source 1

The Treaty of Brest-Litovsk, 1 March 1918.

■ Trotsky did not want to sign the treaty. Suggest why. Why did Lenin think it was necessary to sign it?

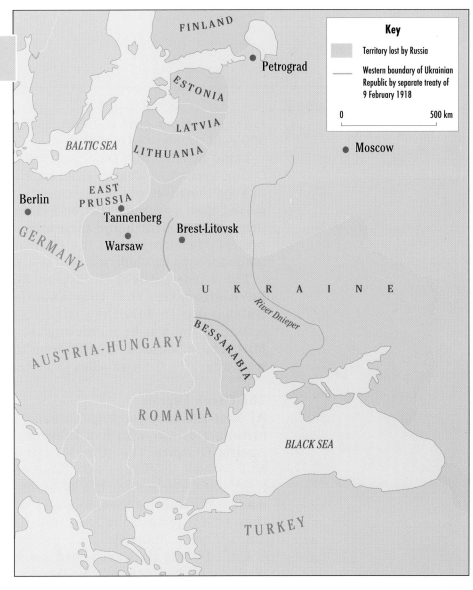

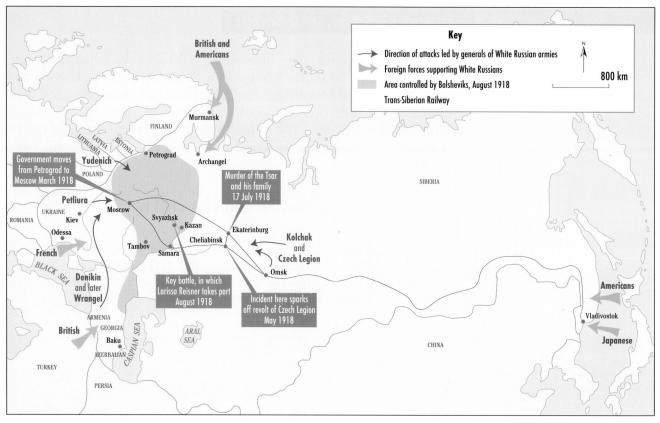

Source 2

The Russian Civil War 1918–1921.

railways, 74 per cent of its iron ore and coal, and paid a fine of 300 gold roubles to Germany.

Lenin insisted that they had to sign the treaty to stop Germany taking over all of Russia. Even so, they did not trust the Germans to keep their side of the agreement. In March 1918 the Bolsheviks moved their government from Petrograd to Moscow. On 5 March they gave the British and their allies permission to land troops to protect Murmansk from the Germans. On 4 April the Japanese landed troops in Vladivostok.

The Brest-Litovsk Treaty so disgusted the Left Socialist Revolutionaries that they abandoned their support for the Bolsheviks. In July they tried to provoke the Germans into restarting the war by murdering the German Ambassador, Count Mirbach, in Moscow. By this time the enemies of the Bolsheviks were attacking from all sides (Source 2). A civil war had begun.

The Czech Legion

At first the most serious threat came from 42,000 Czech ex-prisoners of war who had been captured in the fighting against Austria-Hungary. This 'Czech Legion' and other prisoners of war had decided to change sides and were being taken to France to fight the Germans on the Western Front. German submarines made it difficult for them to travel via Murmansk. So in May 1918 they set off to take the long way round, via Vladivostok on the Trans-Siberian Railway.

Until 14 May the Czechs had no intention of taking sides in the civil war. A bad decision by Trotsky changed this. At the railway station of Cheliabinsk, a Hungarian prisoner of war threw an iron bar at a Czech standing on the platform and badly hurt him. A fight broke out. The Cheliabinsk Soviet arrested a number of Czech soldiers. Their comrades used force to rescue them. When he heard about this, Trotsky ordered the Soviets along the railway to disarm the Czechs.

The furious Czechs rebelled and took over the entire Trans-Siberian railway. The Bolsheviks lost control of the cities along the railway. Protected by the 'Czech Legion', enemies of the Bolsheviks known as the 'Whites' set up rival governments. Among the most important of these was the Committee of the Constituent Assembly (Komuch) based in Samara.

The murder of the Tsar and his family

The former Tsar and his family were held prisoner at Ekaterinburg (see Source 2). It was feared that the Czech Legion might rescue them. A squad of Cheka took over from their guards and shot the royal family on 17 July 1918. Trotsky later explained why the Bolsheviks murdered the Tsar and his family:

Source 3

Trotsky, Diary, 9 April 1935.

The execution of the Tsar's family was needed not only to frighten, horrify and instill a sense of hopelessness in the enemy, but also to shake up our own ranks, to show that there was no retreating, that ahead lay either total victory or total doom.

Terror!

On 22 November 1917 Lenin wrote in the Bolshevik newspaper, *Pravda*:

Source 4

Pravda, 22 November 1917.

We want to transform the government into an instrument for enforcing the will of the people. We want to organise violence in the name of the interests of the workers.

In August 1918 a Socialist Revolutionary, Fanny Kaplan, shot and badly wounded Lenin. The Cheka responded with terror and extreme cruelty. They tortured, mutilated and murdered their victims who included priests, officers in the armed forces, and anyone who showed signs of opposition or resistance. They took hostages and executed them in revenge for attacks on Bolshevik leaders. One Cheka leader told his officers

Source 5

N. Avdeev et al, *Revolution in 1917: A Soviet Chronicle*, 1923–1927.

We are not waging war against individual persons. We are exterminating the bourgeoisie as a class. During the investigation, do not look for evidence that the accused acted in deed or word against Soviet power. The first questions that you ought to put are: To what class does he belong? What is his origin? What is his education or profession? ... In this lies the significance and essence of the terror.

It is said that between 1917 and 1923 the Cheka killed over 200,000 people. By 1922 they had built 190 concentration camps for 85,000 of their victims who survived.

Terror against the peasants

The Bolsheviks' strongest support came from the towns and cities. Food was essential to keep their support. When Lenin sent armed Bolsheviks into the countryside to confiscate their food, the peasants resisted fiercely. Lenin's answer to this was to turn other peasants against those who refused to hand over their grain. He called these peasants *kulaks* ('tight-fisted') and told workers in August 1918:

Source 6

Lenin, *Complete Collected Works*, 1955.

... These bloodsuckers have grown rich during the war on the people's want .... These spiders have grown fat at the expense of peasants .... These leeches have drunk the blood of workers, growing richer the more the worker starved in the cities and the factories .... Merciless war against these *kulaks*! Death to them!

However, it was hard to tell the difference between a *kulak* and an ordinary peasant – all were desperately poor. Lenin's land decree had won the Bolsheviks support from the peasants; now they lost it. The Bolsheviks even took the grain needed for sowing for the next crop. The result was such a terrible famine that there was cannibalism.

Terror against the Church

Lenin used the famine to attack another Bolshevik enemy, the Church:

Source 7

A letter from Lenin to the Politburo, 19 March 1922.

Right now when people are being eaten in famine-stricken areas, we can carry out the confiscation of Church valuables with the most furious and ruthless energy ... we must crush their resistance with such cruelty that they will not forget it for decades.

As the propaganda painting opposite shows (Source 8), the Christian Church was not the only religion seen as the enemy.

The Red Army

Trotsky created a 'Red Army' to save the Bolsheviks from defeat by the 'White Armies'. He used professional army officers to organise it. Political commissars were chosen to work with the officers and to execute them if they were not loyal. In some cases they used officers' families as hostages. These political commissars replaced the 'soldiers committees'. Trotsky made sure that Red Army soldiers were better fed than almost anyone else. He brought back the death penalty and made it compulsory for men to join the Red Army. Source 9 is a comment on his ruthlessness.

Source 8

An anti-religious cartoon from the 1920s. It mocks the major religions in the Soviet Union. The Holy Ghost is shown as a flying purse wearing a capitalist top hat..

■ Which religions are represented here?

Source 9

A poster of 1919 shows Trotsky as the Ogre of the Kremlin.

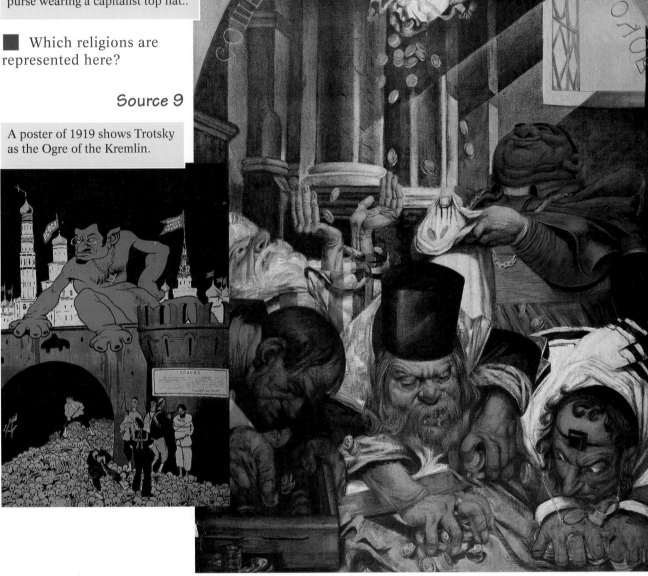

■ What different criticisms of Trotsky are made in this cartoon (clues: the Star of David around his neck; human bones; colours)?

The support of women

Without the support of women the Bolsheviks would not have won the civil war. Thousands dug trenches, built fortifications, fought and died for the Bolsheviks. They worked for the Party's political departments as secret agents and spies, and helped make propaganda. Popular speakers like Konkordia Samoilovna and Alexandra Kollontai gave talks to soldiers on the battlefield.

Larissa Reisner was the first Bolshevik woman commissar. In August 1918 White forces captured Kazan on the River Volga only 650 kilometres away from Moscow. To survive, the Bolsheviks had to defend the town of Svyanzhsk on the road to Moscow. Trotsky warned that if any unit retreated the commissar would be shot, then the commander. At Svyazhsk (see Source 2) Larissa Reisner fought with a rifle on the frontline to stop the advance of the White and Czech armies.

Source 10

Larissa Reisner, *Letters from the Front*, 1919.

> Those who slept on the floor, on straw strewn with broken glass, were afraid of nothing, with almost no hope of victory ... each hour of life had the fullness and freshness of some miracle. A plane came to drop bombs on the station; the sickening bark of machine guns came nearer....

War Communism

The ruthless methods used by the Bolsheviks during the civil war to control industries and food supplies were later called War Communism.

Source 11

Soviet poster: 'Woman! Learn the three R's! Mother, if only you were literate, you would help me.' 88 per cent Russian women could not read or write.

War Communism began with the nationalisation of industry. All privately-owned factories with more than ten workers were put under government control. A Supreme Council of National Economy (*Vesenkha*) was set up to decide what each factory should produce. In the factories, workers were kept under strict control. Strikes were illegal. In the countryside, peasants were made to give their surplus food to the government. They could not sell it for a profit because private trading was banned. In the cities, food was strictly rationed. Finally, the government allowed money to lose its value through inflation. It also abolished money payments such as rents, fares and postal charges. In place of money people bartered goods.

War Communism succeeded in one respect: it kept the Red Army supplied with food and weapons, and so helped the Bolsheviks win the civil war. As you will find out, however, it led in the long term to a terrible famine.

The defeat of the White Armies

In the autumn of 1919 the White Armies again seemed close to victory (Source 2). By 14 October General Deniken's cavalry was only 300 kilometres south-west of Moscow, Kolchak was closing in on the Eastern Front, and on 22 October Yudenich reached the outskirts of Petrograd (Source 2).

Trotsky rushed to Petrograd to take personal command. The Bolshevik already in command there was Zinoviev. Trotsky later described him as 'panic personified'. A week later Trotsky helped organise a successful counter-attack forcing Deniken and Kolchak to retreat. This was the turning point in the civil war.

The White Armies did not have back-up supplies. They fed themselves by looting, which turned peasants against them. They fought under separate commands and huge distances separated them, making communication and teamwork difficult. They also lost the support of their foreign allies. The British, French, American and Japanese had landed troops in Russia to prevent the Germans from capturing weapons and supplies they had sent to Russia. They also wanted Russia to start fighting the Germans again. This was no longer necessary after the Germans surrendered in November 1918. During 1919 most foreign troops left Russia. Only the Japanese, who wanted more power in the Far East, stayed longer.

Source 12

Soviet political poster of 1918. The sword of the Red Army cuts off the advance of the White Russian armies led by Kolchak, Yudenich and Deniken before they reach the Donetsk basin.

Stalin's war

Zinoviev was not the only Bolshevik leader to clash with Trotsky. After the small part he had played in the October Revolution, Stalin seemed determined to make a name for himself too. His men hijacked grain on its way to feed the starving city of Baku. He justified this by saying:

Source 13

From M. McCaulay, *The Soviet Union since 1917*, 1981.

If we lose Baku, it is nothing. We shall take it again within a few months or a year at the most. If we lose Moscow, we lose everything. Then the revolution is over.

Stalin's interference in the defence of Tsaritsyn in October 1918, however, so irritated Trotsky that he sent a telegram to Lenin complaining that the activities of Stalin were wrecking his plans.

Lenin recalled Stalin but in 1920 gave him the job of political commissar on the south-west front in a brief war with Poland. At first, under the brilliant young Red Commander, Tukachevsky, the Red Army did well. However, the Polish Army, led by Pilsudski, shattered the Red Army before it reached Warsaw. Tukachevsky blamed Stalin for not coming to his aid.

Questions

1 **a** What different roles did each of the following play in helping the Bolsheviks win the civil war: Lenin; Trotsky; the Cheka; women; War Communism?
b Which do you consider played the most important role? Explain your answer.

2 Which of the following armies were the greatest threat to the Bolsheviks: the Czech Legion; the White armies; the British, French, American and Japanese 'armies of intervention'? Explain your answer.

3 How did the civil war affect the relationships that Zinoviev and Stalin had with Trotsky?

4.4 Lenin's last years

Lenin had achieved power by force rather than by popularity. To continue in power he had to keep the loyalty of his supporters and improve the economic conditions of the Russian peoples. At the same time Lenin needed to strengthen the control of the Communist Party over the Empire. The final part of this unit examines Lenin's solutions to these problems: the replacement of War Communism by a New Economic Policy and the appointment of Joseph Stalin as General Secretary of the Communist Party. The first solution was a temporary retreat from Communism; the second solution he came to regret.

Why did Lenin introduce a New Economic Policy?

By the end of 1920 the Bolsheviks had begun to lose the support of even their closest followers. Six years of war had ruined the economy and brought famine. In the cities thousands of hungry, orphaned children wandered the streets, scavenging and thieving.

Strikes, mutinies and rebellion
In Petrograd workers went on strike. Meanwhile, at the naval base of Kronstadt, sailors of the Baltic Fleet mutinied. Most of these sailors had been strong Bolshevik supporters. They demanded democracy and an end to War Communism.

Then peasants turned on the Bolsheviks. During the civil war some peasants had joined bandit armies called the 'Greens' who attacked both White and Red Armies. In 1921 an army of about 20,000 Greens led a revolt against the Bolsheviks in the region of Tambov. They pulled up railway lines, started fires and hunted down Bolsheviks, often torturing them before murdering them.

Trotsky ordered the 27-year-old General Tukachevsky to lead 60,000 Red Army soldiers across the winter ice linking Petrograd to the Kronstadt naval base. They crushed the mutiny but paid a heavy price. 10,000 Red Army soldiers died in savage fighting which lasted from 7–18 March 1921. Shortly after this Tukachevsky and his soldiers went into action against the Greens at Tambov. These untrained peasants were no match for the Red Army who shot whole groups of them in cold blood and sent entire villages into exile.

The New Economic Policy (NEP)
With growing alarm Lenin realised that the Bolsheviks could not go on like this and survive in power. In March 1921, at the Tenth Party Congress, he announced a New Economic Policy, saying:

Source 1

Lenin, *Complete Collected Works*, Vol. 32, 1957.

We know that so long as there is no revolution in other countries, only agreement with the peasantry can save the socialist revolution in Russia.

The NEP allowed peasants to sell surplus food and make a profit; the more they produced the less tax they had to pay. People could own small businesses again. Money became trusted again as a way of paying instead of using payment in kind.

The rise of Joseph Stalin

After 1921 anyone who stood up to Lenin and the Communist Party was treated as an outlaw. Inside the party Lenin banned arguments and splits. The Central Executive Committee ruled the party. Inside it a small group close to Lenin, the Politburo, took the important decisions. Another group, the Orgburo, did the organising, and the Secretariat carried out the decisions. The Secretariat made sure that the government, Sovnarkom, did what the Communist Party told it to do. Lenin was Chairman of Sovnarkom and appointed leading members of the party to it.

Source 2

How the Communist Party controlled the government.

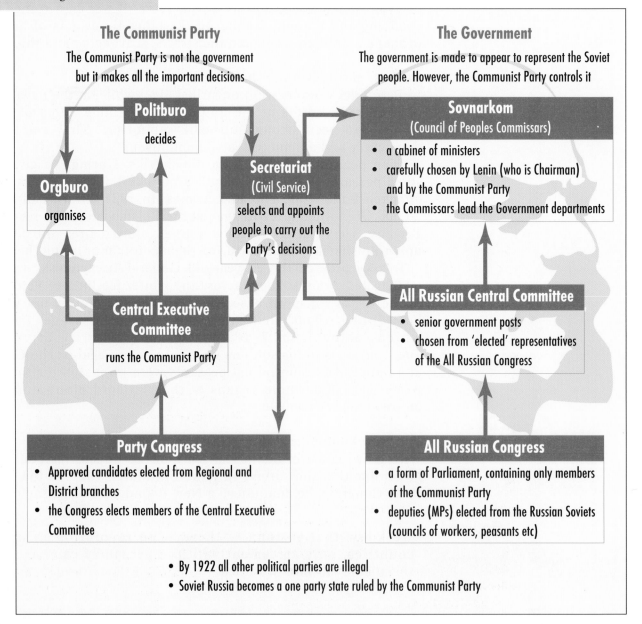

The Communist Party

The Communist Party is not the government but it makes all the important decisions

The Government

The government is made to appear to represent the Soviet people. However, the Communist Party controls it

Politburo

decides

Orgburo

organises

Secretariat
(Civil Service)

selects and appoints people to carry out the Party's decisions

Sovnarkom
(Council of Peoples Commissars)

- a cabinet of ministers
- carefully chosen by Lenin (who is Chairman) and by the Communist Party
- the Commissars lead the Government departments

Central Executive Committee

runs the Communist Party

All Russian Central Committee

- senior government posts
- chosen from 'elected' representatives of the All Russian Congress

Party Congress

- Approved candidates elected from Regional and District branches
- the Congress elects members of the Central Executive Committee

All Russian Congress

- a form of Parliament, containing only members of the Communist Party
- deputies (MPs) elected from the Russian Soviets (councils of workers, peasants etc)

- By 1922 all other political parties are illegal
- Soviet Russia becomes a one party state ruled by the Communist Party

In 1923 one of Lenin's favourites was Joseph Stalin. Between 1917 and 1922 he gave Stalin three important jobs which made him very powerful (People's Commissar for Nationalities, Head of Workers' and Peasants' Inspectorate, and Liaison Officer between the Politburo and Orgburo). But Lenin needed someone loyal and trustworthy to see that the decisions of the party were carried out. He chose Stalin to be General Secretary – head of the Secretariat. The General Secretary appointed the people who carried out the decisions of the Politburo. This job allowed Stalin to look at all the personal files of the party members.

Nobody thought he was a danger. Trotsky described him as a 'grey blur'. However, by 1923 Lenin had second thoughts about Stalin:

Source 3

From a collection of dictated notes known as Lenin's Testament.

Since he became General Secretary, Comrade Stalin has concentrated enormous power in his hands, and I am not sure that he will always know how to use that power with sufficient caution ....

Lenin was shocked by the brutal methods Stalin used to force Georgia to give up all independence and accept direct rule from Moscow. He began to worry about the fact that Stalin was increasing his power by giving top jobs to his own followers and friends. Trotsky noticed:

Source 4

Trotsky, *Stalin: An Appraisal of the Man and his Influence*, 1947.

Right now he is organising around himself the sneaks of the party.

Stalin's own secretary caught him listening in to the conversations of his colleagues on the Kremlin telephone network.

After suffering three strokes between May 1922 and December 1923, Lenin died. However, before he died he had his views on Stalin written down so that the other Communist leaders could read them (Source 3). Stalin knew what was in this document before it was read out. This gave him time to plan what to do.

Lenin's disciple?

At Lenin's funeral people wept and queued in their thousands to pay their last respects. Stalin helped carry the coffin. Petrograd was renamed Leningrad.

Stalin knew that images are important. The Russian people were used to a Tsar acting as a father figure blessed by the Russian Orthodox Church. After 1917 Lenin had become a new father figure. Portraits of Lenin like Source 5 were put on show instead of religious icons. After 1922, however, the public rarely saw Lenin in person because he now looked very different.

It is thought that it was Stalin's idea to embalm Lenin and place him near the Kremlin Wall for the public to visit. Archaeologists had recently found the tomb of the Egyptian Pharaoh,

Source 5

Poster of Lenin, 1967. Notice the strong image.

Source 6

A photograph of Lenin taken shortly before he died. Photographs which showed him to be very ill were censored until 1992.

Tutenkhamun. There was a lot of interest in how the Egyptians preserved the bodies of their pharaohs and worshipped them as gods.

The favourite to replace Lenin was Trotsky. He was on sick leave when Lenin died and missed the funeral. His excuse was that Stalin had tricked him by giving the wrong date. Other Bolshevik leaders like Kamenev and Zinoviev hated Trotsky and did not want him as their leader. Kamenev read Lenin's Testament (the document containing his wishes) to the leaders of the party in secret before the opening of the Twelfth Congress of Soviets. Stalin's secretary, Bazhanov remembers:

Source 7

B. Bazhanov, *With Stalin in the Kremlin*, 1930.

A painful confusion paralysed the audience, Stalin ... felt himself small and pitiable .... In spite of his self-control and enforced calm one could clearly see from his face that his fate was in the balance.

The leaders decided to let Stalin keep his job. It was a dreadful mistake.

Questions

1 Why was Lenin forced to abandon War Communism?

2 In what ways was the New Economic Policy a step backward from Communism?

3 Why did the General Secretary of the Communist Party become so powerful?

4 For what reasons did the Bolshevik leaders ignore Lenin's wish to remove Stalin from the job of General Secretary?

Review

Look again at the picture from Eisenstein's film, *October* (Source 4 on page 52). Eisenstein was looking forward to the first public showing of this film of the October Revolution in 1927 when he was ordered to cut out the parts which showed Trotsky. At that time there was a fierce struggle for power between the Bolshevik leaders. They ganged up on Trotsky to stop him from taking Lenin's place.

Source 1

Lenin making a speech in 1920. Notice Trotsky and Kamenev standing below him to the right.

Now look at Sources 1 and 2. It is said 'the camera never lies'. Is this true? Compare the two photographs. Are they the same or can you spot the difference? The men missing from the second photograph (Source 2) are Trotsky and, behind him, his brother-in-law, Kamenev. Stalin had them 'removed' from the picture.

1 Look carefully through this unit and list as many things as you can that Trotsky contributed to the October Revolution and the Bolshevik victory in the civil war.

2 a Soviet histories of this period written after Stalin came to power do not mention the part played by Trotsky. Write a few sentences which in a similar way draw attention to the parts played by Lenin, Stalin and the women mentioned in this unit rather than Trotsky.
b What are the dangers of writing history like this?
c Suggest ways you can question, challenge and check up on interpretations of history to avoid such dangers.

Source 2

Lenin making a speech in 1920. This is the same photograph as Source 1 but what has happened to Trotsky and Kamenev?

Unit 5 • The Red Tsar

After Lenin died, the seven members of the Communist Party Politburo said that they would share power. They were Trotsky, Zinoviev, Kamenev, Stalin, Bukharin, Rykov and Tomsky. The truth is that a power struggle took place between them.

Stalin started with the advantage that his rivals saw each other as more of a threat than Stalin himself. They underestimated the power he had as General Secretary to control party members and to know everything that was happening. This allowed Stalin to build alliances, isolate his rivals and destroy them one by one. By 1929 it was clear that he was the new leader of Russia.

Stalin has been compared to the ruthless Tsar, Ivan the Terrible. Stalin's methods, like Ivan the Terrible's, were autocratic and cruel. He was determined to make the Russian Empire into a Communist state and a great world power. The first part of this unit focuses on the methods Stalin used to bring about a second revolution which transformed farming and industry.

5.1 Stalin's revolution

Stalin said in 1931:

Source 1

J. Stalin, *Problems of Leninism*, 1945.

We are fifty or a hundred years behind the advanced countries. We must make good this distance in ten years. Either we do it, or we shall go under.

■ Suggest what Stalin had to fear from 'the advanced countries'?

There were two problems to solve:

1 The peasants were not producing enough food to feed the Soviet Union and make money to invest in industry.
2 Industries were not growing fast enough.

Stalin's answer to the first problem was collectivisation. He ordered all peasants to give up privately or communally owned farms and put them together into *kolkhozy* (collective farms) or *sovkhozy* (state farms).

The answer to the second problem was to plan ambitious targets for industrial growth for every five years: 1928–1932; 1933–1937; 1938–1941 (interrupted by war); 1946–1950; 1951–1955.

Did collectivisation succeed?

To make a collective farm (*kolkhoz*) peasants had to pool their privately-owned fields, animals and equipment. Instead of making profits by selling their produce at market, peasants now sold their

Source 2

Anti-*kulak* cartoon. Notice the priest comforting the *kulak* and the sympathetic journalist seen at the window – these were the *kulak*'s allies.

■ Look at Source 2. Who was blamed for resisting collectivisation and why?

Source 3

A victim of the famine of 1932–1934. Few people living in the West knew about the famine at the time.

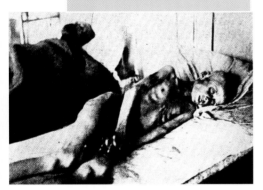

produce to the government for a fixed, low price. They received wages for their work.

Collective farms contained 50 to 100 families, together farming an average 450 hectares of land. 'Machine Tractor Stations' in each area, one for every 40 farms, provided tractors, drivers and other farming equipment to help the collectives plough and harvest the land.

Stalin knew that the richest peasants – those who had most to lose – would resist his plans for collectivisation. He therefore continued where Lenin had left off before he started the New Economic Policy (see page 58) by launching an attack on the '*kulaks*'. Stalin accused *kulaks* of hoarding grain to force up prices so that they could make a profit. Squads of armed town workers went into the countryside in 1928–1929 to set up road blocks, and break into peasant homes and grain stores to take away food and grain by force. They took the sowing grain needed for the next harvest.

Peasants fiercely resisted collectivisation. They preferred to slaughter their animals, feast and burn their homes rather than let the collectives have them. Stalin responded by deporting over 10 million peasants to forced labour camps in the Urals and Siberia where 3 million died.

Famine!

In 1932 there was a poor harvest and a shortage of food in the countryside. This led to a famine which lasted until 1934. However, the famine did not have entirely natural causes. Stalin deliberately allowed this disaster to happen.

Stalin was expecting to go to war with Japan in the Far East. He wanted to build stocks to feed the Red Army and so sent in squads from the Communist Party and the secret police (now changed from Cheka to OGPU) to seize more food. Soon there was no more food to find in the countryside. Soldiers guarded grain stores and let the grain rot rather than feed the hungry. The Soviet Union even sold grain abroad to buy machinery and raw materials for industries rather than give it to the starving. Over 7 million people died. Carts piled with bodies went around villages picking up the dead for mass burials. People ate earthworms, the bark of trees, mice, ants and even their own children to survive. One Ukrainian said of his neighbour:

Source 4

Mykola Pishy, a Ukrainian interviewed for the Thames Television series, *Stalin*, 1990.

Ivan was a good specialist – a joiner, a tailor, a shoe-maker – a good fellow who could turn his hand to anything. But the famine was awful and he got to the end of his tether. He was so hungry that he killed his child, and ate the meat.

By 1934 Stalin had won his battle with the peasants. He later described it to Winston Churchill as worse than any battle fought against Nazi Germany. But at what cost did he win it?

Source 5

Figures based on Soviet statistics.

1 The numbers of livestock in the USSR (in millions)

	Horses	Cattle	Pigs	Sheep and goats
1928	33	70	26	146
1932	15	34	9	42

2 The amount of food sold in the towns and cities (in kilograms)

	Bread	Potatoes	Meat and lard	Butter
1928	250.4	141.1	24.8	1.35
1932	214.6	125.0	11.2	0.7

Did industrialisation succeed?

These were the targets of the First Five Year Plan:

- increase agricultural production by 55 per cent;
- increase industrial production by 180 per cent;
- increase investment by 228 per cent;
- increase sales of products by 70 per cent.

Posters like Source 6 captured the imagination of young Communists. Fired with enthusiasm, young workers braved the cold and primitive conditions of the Ural Mountains to live in tents while they built the biggest iron and steel works in the world at Magnitogorsk.

Western eyes turned to the Soviet Union in admiration. There were other remarkable achievements such as the Dnieper dam to provide hydro-electricity and new industrial centres in the Kuzbass and the Volga. Stalin went out of his way to praise and

Source 6

This poster says: ' We are the industrial plan for fulfilling the five year plan in four years against religion', 1930.

Source 7

Magnitogorsk, a tiny village in the Ural Mountains, became an industrial city with.a huge steel works part of which is shown in this photograph.

reward model workers like the Ukrainian coal miner Alexei Stakhanov who, it was said, proved it was possible to cut 102 tonnes of coal a day instead of the seven tonnes each miner had to cut.

The First Five Year Plan was hailed as a stunning success. It is difficult to believe the official statistics; desperate managers fiddled the books. However, Western experts believe Source 8 to be close to the real figures:

Source 8

A. Nove, *An Economic History of the Soviet Union,* 1969.

Results of the First Five Year Plan

Product (million tonnes)	1928 (original target)	1932 (revised target)	1932 (what was achieved)
Coal	35	75	64
Oil	11.7	21.7	21.1
Iron ore	6.7	20.2	12.1
Pig iron	3.2	10	6.2

Much was achieved despite disappointments. The Second and Third Five Year Plans continued to give priority to heavy industries like coal, steel, oil and electricity (Source 9).

Source 9

Adapted from E. Zaleski, *Stalinist Planning for Economic Growth, 1933–1952*, 1980.

Results of the Second and Third Five Year Plans (production figures based on Soviet and Western sources)

	1932	1937	1940
Coal (million tonnes)	64	128	150
Steel (million tonnes)	6	18	18
Oil (million tonnes)	21	26	26
Electricity (million kWs)	20	80	90

The promise that the Second Five Year Plan would spend more on producing goods to buy in shops, housing and better wages was not kept. As Source 10 shows, the money was spent instead on defence, which increased its share of all money invested:

Source 10

A. Nove, *An Economic History of the USSR*, 1969.

The share of all spending on defence

1933	1937	1940
3.4%	16.5%	32.6%

The human cost

It was impossible to build enough new houses for all the millions of peasants who poured into towns and on to construction sites. Overcrowded, rundown buildings with shared kitchens, bathrooms and toilets became home for most families.

Discipline, punishment and rewards

In 1929 factories started working seven days a week. On any day a fifth of workers had the day off. For Christians, Jews and Muslims this made it difficult to attend places of worship. Families found it difficult to spend days together. From 1931 all industrial and transport workers had to obey strict rules or risk going to prison. Each worker had a record book. Anyone caught stealing after August 1932 was sentenced to death. Workers absent from work for only one day were immediately sacked. It was not possible to find work or change a job without an internal passport.

Some workers were better off than others. From 1931 skilled workers were paid better, given better homes, better food and were allowed to go into special shops. Town workers were better off than those on the collective and state farms who did not have social security or internal passports.

Spies and saboteurs?

Stalin ran the economy as if the Soviet Union was at war and there was a constant state of emergency. He believed more workers were needed in industries. Eager to escape

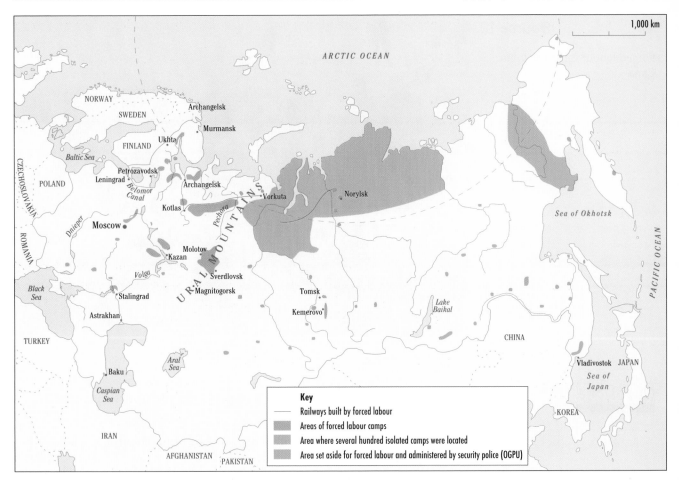

Source 11

The network of labour camps run by Gulag.

Key
— Railways built by forced labour
▨ Areas of forced labour camps
▨ Area where several hundred isolated camps were located
▨ Area set aside for forced labour and administered by security police (OGPU)

collectivisation, 17 million peasants poured into towns and on to construction sites. These were not skilled workers. Factories were short of basic tools. There were accidents; machinery got broken. Spies and saboteurs were said to be everywhere.

In 1928 55 engineers working in the Shakhty coal-mines in the Donbass were accused of sabotaging equipment and organising accidents and were put on trial. The son of one of them was among those who demanded the death penalty. Despite their innocence, five were shot.

Gulag

Some of the tasks set by the Five-Year Plans were so big that there were not enough workers to do them. Prisoners in prison camps were made to do such work. Their prisons thus became labour camps.

In 1930 the secret police (OGPU) set up a special department to run the labour camps. It was called Gulag (chief administration of camps). By 1935 some 5 million prisoners from these camps all over the Soviet Union worked on building projects. Source 12 shows one example.

Stalin wanted the Navy to be able to reach the White Sea from the Baltic through inland waterways. Between 1931 and 1933, 250,000 slave labourers built the Belomor Canal by hand with picks and wheelbarrows (Source 12).

Source 12

Forced labour on the Belomor Canal.

Questions

1 Did collectivisation solve the problem of food shortages in towns? Explain your answer.

2 How can Sources 8 and 9 be used to suggest that the Five-Year Plans were successful?

3 How can the information on pages 73 and 74 be used to suggest that the Soviet people paid a high price for the industrialisation of their country?

4 Describe the methods used and working conditions shown in the building of the Belomor canal.

5 Suggest the different reasons why so many people were sent to labour camps.

5.2 Hero worship, artists, writers, musicians and education

After coming to power in 1917, the Bolsheviks encouraged artists, writers, musicians and film-makers to experiment with new forms of creativity. Source 1 is an example of the new directions taken by artists. One of the Bolshevik leaders explained the party's attitude to the arts:

Source 1

Trotsky, *Literature and Revolution*, 1923.

In the sphere of art it is not the party's business to command. It can and should protect, encourage and merely offer indirect guidance.

The enthusiastic outpouring of new art, literature, films and music in the 1920s made the Soviet Union one of the world's leading centres of the arts. In the 1930s, however, Stalin reversed the party's cultural policy. Artists, writers and musicians now had to follow a policy of 'socialist realism'. Stalin wanted writers and

Source 2

A painting by P. Finolov. Finolov developed a principle of painting called, 'universal flowering'. Instead of normal compositions he used minute brushstrokes to represent every atom of nature.

Source 3

Socialist realist painting, *Higher and Higher* by S.V. Ryangina.

artists to produce work that could easily be recognised and remembered: stories with heroes and heroines and happy endings; paintings which inspired heroic thoughts. He wanted music to be easy to listen to and even to hum.

Why did Stalin want such a dramatic change in the culture of the Soviet Union?

What were the aims of socialist realism?

Painters and photographers

One of the aims of socialist realism can be seen in paintings like Source 3. The purpose of paintings like these was to inspire men and women to work together to build socialism. Photographers too were expected to play their part. Source 4 is a photomontage, made by sticking together different pieces of photograph. Its purpose was to encourage hero-worship.

Writers

Stalin read a great deal. He thought of writers as 'the engineers of the soul'. Some, like the poet Myakovsky, saw what was coming and committed suicide in despair in 1930. From 1932 writers had to belong to the Union of Soviet Writers.

What Stalin did not want was criticism. The poet Osip Mandelstam dared to make up a poem about Stalin:

Source 4

A photomontage of Stalin and the peoples of the Soviet Union.

Source 5

O. Mandelstam's poem about Stalin, 1933.

■ Which lines of the poem do you recognise are about Stalin and why?

All we hear is the Kremlin mountaineer,
The murderer and peasant slayer

His fingers are fat as grubs
And the words, final as lead weights, fall from his lips

His cockroach whiskers leer
And his top boots gleam

Around him a rabble of thin-necked leaders –
Fawning half men for him to play with.

Though Mandelstam did not write this down an informer told the secret police about it. They arrested him in 1934. He died in a labour camp. It was safer to write poems like this:

Source 6

A. O. Avdienko, in *Pravda*, August 1936.

O great Stalin, O leader of the peoples,
Thou who broughtest man to birth ...
... Thou who makest bloom the spring,
Thou who makest vibrate the musical chords ...

The writer Avdienko went so far as to say:

Source 7

A. O. Avdienko, in *Pravda*, February 1935.

When the woman I love gives me a child, the first word I will teach it shall be 'Stalin'.

Musicians

Stalin loved music. Dmitri Shostakovich was one of the most famous composers in Russia. In 1934 his opera, *Lady Macbeth of Mtsensk*, was a huge success and ran for two years. In 1936 Stalin and Molotov went to see it. Shortly afterwards Shostakovich read a criticism of it in *Pravda* calling the opera 'muddle and chaos'. All of a sudden he was 'an enemy of the people'.

Afraid for his life and family, Shostakovich withdrew his latest work, the Fourth Symphony, from rehearsal. In 1937 he presented a Fifth Symphony with the sub-title, 'A Soviet Artist's Practical Creative Reply to Just Criticism'. It was a tremendous success. It appeared to be just what Stalin wanted, especially the climax which seemed to be 'rejoicing'. However, Shostakovich was really taking a huge risk. Many of those in the Leningrad audience who had suffered under Stalin understood its real message. Many wept during the slow movement because of what they recognised. Shostakovich later wrote about the climax:

Source 8

Solomon Volkov, ed., *Testimony: The Memoirs of Shostakovich*, 1979.

I think it is clear to everyone what happens in the Fifth. The Rejoicing is forced, created under threat .... It is as if someone were beating you over the head with a stick and saying, 'Your business is rejoicing, your business is rejoicing' .... You have to be a complete oaf not to hear that.

Education

Teachers taught that Stalin was the 'Great Leader (*vohzd*) and Genius of all time'. Children learned Stalin's version of history. The Revolution had brought more informal and creative lessons in schools. Stalin stopped all that. He brought back uniforms, compulsory pigtails for girls, single-sex classes, formal tests and examinations. He stopped 'project' work and he introduced a core curriculum in mathematics, science, a foreign language, history and geography. Those who wanted to stay at secondary school for more than three years had to pay fees.

Questions

1 What do Sources 3 and 4 tell us about the kind of paintings Stalin wanted people to see and about how Stalin liked to be seen?

2 **a** What do you think Stalin meant by describing writers as the 'engineers of the soul'?
b How does Stalin's view compare with Trotsky's (Source 1)?

3 What does the story of Shostakovich's Fifth Symphony suggest about the difficulty of enforcing 'socialist realism' in music?

5.3   Purges

Stalin had good reason to fear that he had made enemies. From 1936 he began 'purges' of so-called 'enemies of the people'. 'Purges' meant the systematic elimination of enemies. At first it seemed he dealt only with those known to him personally. There were 'show trials' and executions of old political rivals. What was extraordinary, however, was that his purges went much further: 20 million people in the Russian Empire died and millions more were imprisoned as slave labour in concentration camps.

Why did Stalin's purges go so far?

The immediate background

In the summer of 1932, Ryutin, a senior member of the party, criticised Stalin's policy of collectivisation and Five Year Plans. He passed around a document which described Stalin as:

Source 1

Quoted in *Izvestia Tsk KPSS*, no. 6, 1989.

> the evil genius of the Russian Revolution who, activated by vindictiveness and lust for power, has brought the revolution to the edge of the abyss.

A furious Stalin had Ryutin and his supporters arrested and put on trial. He wanted the death penalty for them but the other members of the Politburo, including his friend Kirov, outvoted Stalin. Instead they expelled Ryutin from the party and exiled him.

The murder of Kirov

Stalin used the Ryutin affair to set an example. The time had come to 'purge' or expel from the party anyone else who might think of criticising him.

He felt the need to do so when the Seventeenth Party Congress was held in 1934. At the Congress, Stalin decided to give his critics and old enemies a chance to confess their mistakes and declare their support for him. Anxious to get back into favour, old rivals like Bukharin and Kamenev queued up to praise Stalin. But Stalin noticed he was not the only one enthusiastically clapped and cheered. The other man the Congress liked was Sergei Kirov, a member of the Politburo. A group asked him to stand for Stalin's job of General Secretary. Kirov refused but even so his days were numbered. On 1 December Kirov was shot dead at his headquarters in Leningrad.

NKVD A new name given to the police in 1934: People's Commissariat of Internal Affairs.

An investigation reported that the killer had acted on the orders of a 'Leningrad opposition centre' linked with Zinoviev and Kamenev who were immediately arrested. Although the murder was actually organised by Stalin, this was the signal for mass arrests. Within a few months the secret police, the NKVD*, had arrested 40,000 people in Leningrad alone.

Source 2

A table of the purges.

Date	The Victims	What happened to them	Crimes accused of
Managers and engineers			
1928	55 engineers from Shakhty mines in Donbas	Public show trial, 5 shot, 49 prison	Sabotage
1930–31	Industrialists	Show trial, prison, 5 death sentences not carried out	Sabotage
	Mensheviks	Show trial, prison	Political crimes
	Bacteriologists, food scientists	Secret trials, several executed	Sabotage, wrecking the economy, spying
1933	Engineers from Metro-Vickers	Show trial, prison; some released	Sabotage, spying
	State farm officials	Secret trials, 70 shot	Sabotage, causing food shortages
Senior Party Leaders			
1932	Ryutin Group	Expelled from Party, exiled	Treason, plotting against Stalin
1934	Kirov	Murdered (probably on Stalin's orders)	None (popular favourite to replace Stalin)
1936	Zinoviev and Kamenev	Show trial, shot	Kirov's murder, links with Trotsky
1937	Pyatakov, Serebryakov,	Show trial, shot	Spying for Germany and Japan
	Radek, Sokolnikov	Sent to labour camps	Spying for Germany and Japan
1938	Bukharin, Rykov, Krestinsky	Show trial, shot	Treason
Other Party Officials			
	Almost every party and state leader in every one of the republics of the USSR	Shot or sent to labour camp	'Bourgeois nationalism', treason
The Armed Forces			
1937–	3 out of 5 Marshals (including Tukhachevsky)	All executed	Treason
	14 out of 16 Army commanders,		
	8 out of 8 Admirals,		
	60 out of 67 Corps commanders,		
	136 out of 199 Divisional commanders,		
	221 out of 397 Brigade commanders		
	11 out of 11 deputy Commissars for defence,	All executed	Treason
	78 out of 80 members of Supreme Military Council		
	Half of the officer corps (35 000)	Shot or imprisoned	Treason
People with foreign connections			
	Diplomats, foreign trade officials, intelligence agents	Shot or sent to labour camps	Spying, treason, sabotage
	Foreign communist leaders in exile in Russia e.g. Bela Kun (Hungary)	Shot or sent to labour camps	Spying, counter-revolution
The Security Services			
1937	Yagoda – head of NKVD	Show trial (with Bukharin), shot	Treason, murder, corruption
	Most senior police officials		
1939	Yezhov (Yagoda's replacement)	Shot	British agent, killing innocent people
Others			
1929–39	Up to 24 million people	Transported to labour camps, 13 million died	Kulaks, criminals, wreckers, failure to inform on others
1934	1 million people mainly in Moscow and Leningrad	Arrested and executed	Links with Kirov's murder
1940	2 million from Baltic states, Bukovina and Latvia	Deported east, most died	Nationals who were 'enemies'
1941	3 million including Germans, Chechens, Crimean Tartars	Deported, one third died	Nationals disloyal to the USSR
1944–46	10 million returning Prisoners of war	Transported to labour camps, 5–6 million died	'Politically contaminated by foreigners'
1947–53	1 million people	Arrested, many died	Political crimes

Source 3

Mass grave found at Cheliabinsk in the Urals in 1989.

The 'Great Purge' of 1936–1938

In 1936 the 'purges' began to accelerate. Stalin needed evidence to get rid of his rivals forever. The NKVD went out at night in vans nicknamed 'black ravens'. The victims were woken up by a knock at the door and taken from their families to the NKVD headquarters in Moscow, a large building called the Lubyanka. The victims were tortured into confessing to crimes they did not do. The most effective torture was to prevent victims from sleeping by continuous questioning by teams of interrogators. This was called the 'conveyor belt method' because it kept up the flow of pressure. Beatings and threats about what the NKVD could do to their families usually did the trick – especially after the age for the death penalty was reduced to include 12-year-old children.

The mostly false evidence gathered by the NKVD was used for three famous show trials between 1936 and 1938 of the old Bolshevik leaders who had fallen out with Stalin (Source 2). These men made remarkable confessions of their guilt and provided evidence to convict each other for everyone to see on film or hear on radio. At the end of their trial the chief prosecutor, Vyshinsky, demanded that 'these mad dogs be shot'.

The climate of terror

To be expelled from the party had cruel consequences. It meant taking away the victim's party card. Without the party card it was impossible to get a job. This punished the whole family. Wives divorced their husbands in order to survive and people avoided those expelled for fear that the same might happen to them.

Source 4

Front page newspaper photograph of Trotsky with an ice-pick through his head.

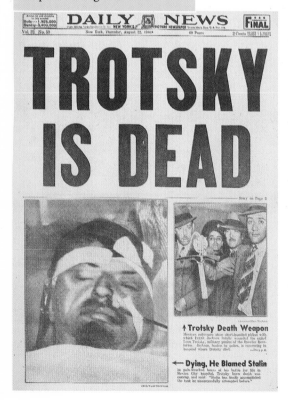

When both parents of one 13-year-old girl were arrested she was turned out on to the street. To survive she had to tell a meeting of Young Pioneers (a communist youth organisation) that her parents were spies and deserved to be shot. No one was safe. Everyone lived in terror and feared informers who were known as *stukachi* ('knockers'). One of the perks of informing was that the informer received the victim's possessions. There were a number of cases of children informing on their parents.

Millions disappeared. Many victims were simply shot in the back of the head after interrogation and taken in vans to be buried in waste ground outside Moscow. Children playing nearby saw them unload the naked bodies. On just one day in December 1938 Stalin and his Prime Minister, Molotov, signed about 30 lists which condemned 3,182 people to death. Hundreds of mass graves (Source 3) have since been discovered.

Stalin's enemies were not safe even if living abroad. On 21 August 1940, one of his agents finally reached Trotsky at his home in Mexico and buried an ice-pick in his head (Source 4).

Questions

1 Suggest possible motives Stalin may have had for organising the murder of Kirov.

2 What did people have to fear from being expelled from the Communist Party?

3 Why do you think the age for the death penalty was reduced to 12?

4 Look at Source 2.
  a What short term consequences for the defence of the Soviet Union were the purges likely to have?
  b Roughly how many people died in the 'purges'?

5 Look at Source 4. Why do you think Stalin went to so much trouble to have Trotsky murdered?

Review

1 a What advantages did Stalin have over his rivals in the struggle for power between 1924 and 1929?
  b By what methods did he win the struggle for power?

2 Examine all the evidence in Unit 5.1.
  a What did Stalin aim to achieve by collectivisation and Five Year Plans?
  b Look back to Unit 2 page 29. Did Stalin succeed where Stolypin failed to solve the problems of farming?
  c In what sense were the economic achievements of Stalin another kind of revolution?
  d In what ways did Stalin's methods of achieving his economic revolution affect the lives of the people of the Soviet Union?

3 Were the kinds of creativity in painting, writing and music which 'socialist realism' allowed art or propaganda? Give reasons for your answer.

4 Study the evidence in Unit 5.3 (pages 78–80). Why do you think Stalin felt the purges were necessary?

5 Is it accurate or misleading to remember Stalin as the 'Red Tsar'? Give reasons to explain your answer.

Unit 6 • Communism and the wider world

6.1 The creation of the Soviet Union

In 1917 the Russian Empire changed hands. Instead of being ruled by an autocratic Tsar who was a Russian Orthodox Christian, a new kind of autocrat who believed in Communism now ruled the Russian Empire: Lenin. As a Communist, Lenin was against having an empire. This section examines how the Bolsheviks tried to transform the Empire into something different which fitted into their ideas of Communism – a Soviet Union. Did they succeed?

Was the Soviet Union just the Russian Empire under a new name?

Source 1

Karl Marx had written that 'any nation which oppresses another can never be free'. So, in 1917 the Bolsheviks said that any nation which wanted to break free could do so. Lenin made

The different stages in the growth of the Soviet Union.

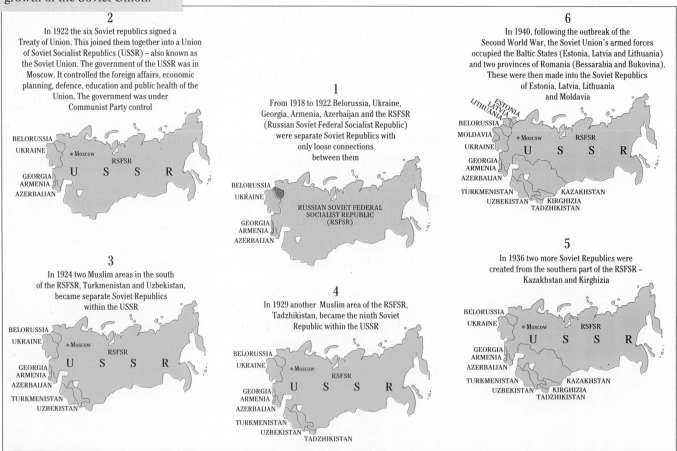

2
In 1922 the six Soviet republics signed a Treaty of Union. This joined them together into a Union of Soviet Socialist Republics (USSR) – also known as the Soviet Union. The government of the USSR was in Moscow. It controlled the foreign affairs, economic planning, defence, education and public health of the Union. The government was under Communist Party control

1
From 1918 to 1922 Belorussia, Ukraine, Georgia, Armenia, Azerbaijan and the RSFSR (Russian Soviet Federal Socialist Republic) were separate Soviet Republics with only loose connections between them

6
In 1940, following the outbreak of the Second World War, the Soviet Union's armed forces occupied the Baltic States (Estonia, Latvia and Lithuania) and two provinces of Romania (Bessarabia and Bukovina). These were then made into the Soviet Republics of Estonia, Latvia, Lithuania and Moldavia

3
In 1924 two Muslim areas in the south of the RSFSR, Turkmenistan and Uzbekistan, became separate Soviet Republics within the USSR

4
In 1929 another Muslim area of the RSFSR, Tadzhikistan, became the ninth Soviet Republic within the USSR

5
In 1936 two more Soviet Republics were created from the southern part of the RSFSR – Kazakhstan and Kirghizia

Source 2

The Soviet Republics painted by Karpov in1924 which contains symbols of the USSR.

Stalin Commissar for Nationalities. His job was to bring together the nations of the old Empire into a union of Soviets.

In 1918 the Bolsheviks changed their name to the Communist Party and formed the Russian Soviet Federal Socialist Republic (RSFSR). They wanted to replace the old ruling class of each nation by the proletariat (the working class). During the civil war the Communists reconquered the parts of the Empire which had chosen independence since 1917 and made them Soviet Republics. Then in 1922 the RSFSR signed a treaty of union with these Soviet Republics to make the Union of Soviet Socialist Republics (USSR) – also known as the Soviet Union.

Each republic was supposed to be free to leave the USSR if it wanted to, but because the Communist Party controlled each republic this was not possible. Stalin became General Secretary of the Communist Party in 1922 and made sure that the leaders of each republic obeyed orders from Moscow.

Questions

1 Look at Source 2. It represents the USSR in 1924 when there were only six republics and contains symbols of the USSR.
a How can you tell that the people represent the six republics?
b What are the six symbols they are carrying on the board?

2 For what reasons could the Soviet Union still be called an empire?

6.2 Religion and nationalities

Source 1

Painting by Nikolai Sysoyev, *Lenin Receiving Eastern Leaders*. Notice Trotsky and Dzerzhinsky standing in the background. Dzerzhinsky was head of the secret police (the Cheka) and had a reputation for fanatical loyalty and ruthlessness. Paintings like this created a leadership cult around Lenin to encourage hero worship and to show which other leaders were close to him.

As the Soviet Union expanded, the different religions and nationalities inside it threatened to pull it apart. This section shows how the Communists tried to unite the Soviet peoples by destroying feelings of separate national identity.

By what methods were the Soviet peoples united?

The creation of a leadership cult

Though it is said that Lenin did not approve of personality cults, paintings like Source 1 appeared and continued to appear in great numbers after his death. The aim was to encourage people to replace religious worship and national feelings with admiration for the Communist leaders and belief in the ideas they stood for.

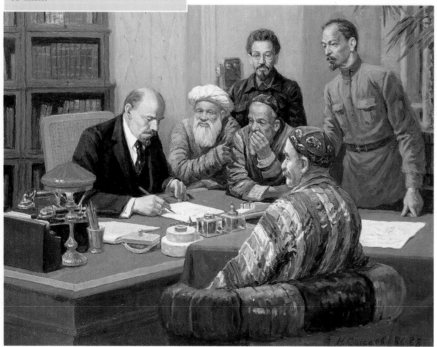

Religious persecution

Persecution of Jews and other minority groups was not new. The Communists, however, also persecuted the two main religious groups, Orthodox Christians and Muslims.

The main Christian Church was the Russian Orthodox Church. In the days of the Tsar Orthodoxy was the official religion. In 1918 the Orthodox Church ceased to be the official church. The Communists took over all Church property and banned religious education outside the family. They took from priests the right to vote, made them pay higher taxes, and gave them lower level ration cards. They stopped their children from having higher education.

Between 1919 and 1921 there was a fierce campaign of anti-religious propaganda; Communists wrecked large numbers of buildings and closed half the monasteries. The Cheka killed eighteen bishops and attacked thousands of priests. From 1929 only registered groups of twenty people over the age of 18 could worship. All worship had to be outside church buildings. It was illegal to convert people to Christianity.

As the Soviet Union expanded, Islam became the other main religion. In the early days tribal Muslim groups in Central Asia formed rebel bands called Bismachi to resist Soviet rule. For this reason the Communists started by being far more tolerant of Muslims than Christians. They promised Muslims:

Source 2

'Bolshevik Declaration to all Toiling Muslims of Russia and the East', 20 November 1917.

Henceforth your beliefs and customs, your national and cultural activities are declared free and inviolate ... know that your rights, like the rights of all the peoples of Russia, are protected by the whole might of the revolution and its organ, the Soviets of the Workers' Soldiers' and Peasants' Deputies.

In the early 1920s the Communists tolerated Muslim law, schools and public rituals. They treated their Mullahs (Muslim teachers) as equal citizens. But by the mid-1920s the Communists had crushed Bismachi resistance. Soon they had closed separate Muslim schools, hospitals and mosques. Only 1,312 were open by 1941 compared with 26,279 in 1912.

■ Why do you think new recruits to the armed forces were deliberately sent a long way from their homeland into ethnically mixed formations?

The destruction of nations

Stalin tried to destroy whole nations by getting rid of national leaders and artists, by attacking religions, by splitting up and deporting nations and by mass murder.

In 1938 national recruitment replaced local recruitment into the armed forces. New recruits were deliberately sent a long way from their homeland into ethnically mixed formations. A future leader of the Soviet Union once said:

Source 3

Brezhnev quoted in G. Hosking, *A History of the Soviet Union*, 1985.

Our army is a ... school of Internationalism.

On the 14 and 15 June 1941 Stalin deported 60,000 Estonians, 34,000 Latvians and 38,000 Lithuanians to Siberia or Central Asia. Before 1941 Stalin split up and widely dispersed a million people from Eastern Poland. During the Second World War he deported whole nations to distant parts of the Soviet Union for collaborating with the enemy. These included:

1941	Volga Germans	1944	Chechens and Ingushi*
1943	Karachai*		Kalmyks
			Balkars*
			Crimean Tartars
			Meskhetians

*Islamic mountain peoples

Questions

1 Marx wrote that 'any nation which oppresses another can never be free'. Why then did the Communists oppress many of the nationalities in the Soviet Union?

2 Why did the Communists persecute both Christians and Muslims?

6.3   The Nazi–Soviet Pact

A map of the world as viewed from the Soviet Union.

A German anti-Communist poster. It says 'Bolshevism will drown the world in blood'.

A. Hitler, *Mein Kampf*, 1924.

J. Stalin, ed., *Leninism*, 1940.

Revolution and civil war left the Soviet Union surrounded by countries whose leaders hated and feared 'Bolshevism' (see Sources 1 and 2). The Soviet Union had three aims in foreign relations:

1 to spread Communism to the rest of the world;
2 to make the Soviet Union strong enough to defend itself;
3 to avoid a war on two fronts: East and West.

The geographical advantages of the Soviet Union were its size and natural resources. The disadvantages were that it shared an enormous land border with many unfriendly countries which was difficult to defend, and that its resources were underdeveloped.

To achieve the first aim Lenin created the Comintern (the Communist International) in 1919. Its purpose was to set up communist parties in each country and help them organise revolutions. To achieve the second aim, Stalin carried out a ruthless economic revolution (see Unit 5.1). To avoid war on two fronts the Soviet Union was prepared to trade, and even make treaties with non-communist countries. As Communists believed that all non-communist governments were bad, the Soviet Union was not choosy. The most astonishing treaty it made was a non-aggression pact with Nazi Germany in August 1939. This section investigates what was so surprising about this and why it happened.

Why did Stalin make a pact with Hitler in 1939?

The rise to power of Hitler

In the year that Lenin died (1924) Adolf Hitler wrote his autobiography, *Mein Kampf* (*My Struggle*). It was more than a story about his life. *Mein Kampf* explained Hitler's ideas and plans for the future. He wanted living space (*lebensraum*) for the German 'master race'. He wrote:

And if we speak of territory in Europe, we can have in mind only Russia and her vassal border states .... The gigantic empire in the East is ready to collapse.

Once in power in 1933, Hitler smashed the German Communist Party and began preparing for war with the Soviet Union. The Soviet Union reacted by joining the League of Nations in 1934. In a speech that year, Stalin said:

Of course we are far from being enthusiastic about the fascist regime in Germany. But fascism is not the issue.... He who wants peace and seeks business-like relations with us will always be welcome.

The success of Stalin's First Five Year Plan inside the Soviet Union so impressed and worried Hitler that he started a plan of his own in 1936. He gave orders that:

Source 5

J. Noakes and G. Pridham, eds, *Nazism 1919–45: A Documentary Reader.*

1 The German armed forces must be operational within four years.
2 The German economy must be fit for war in four years.

Stalin now tried to persuade Britain and France to join an anti-fascist alliance. In 1936, for example, he sent aid to Spain to help the Republicans fight conservative rebels supported by Italy and Germany. However, in the same year Germany, Italy and an old enemy, Japan, agreed to work together against Communism by forming an Anti-Comintern Pact. Fear of being attacked from east

Source 6

A Soviet anti-fascist poster, 1937. It says 'Fascism means famine, fascism means terror, fascism means war'.

Source 7

An American cartoon showing Stalin as the bride and Hitler as the groom in a marriage of convenience.

WONDER HOW LONG THE HONEYMOON WILL LAST?

ФАШИЗМ – ЭТО ГОЛОД,
ФАШИЗМ – ЭТО ТЕРРОР,
ФАШИЗМ – ЭТО ВОЙНА!

and west made Stalin even more desperate for an alliance with Britain and France. Source 6 shows how the Soviet leaders now began to prepare the Soviet people for conflict with Germany.

Germany became more aggressive. The invasion of Austria in 1938 was followed by a threat to expand into Czechoslovakia in the same year. Without involving the Soviet Union, Britain, France and Italy agreed to let Germany take over the German-speaking part of Czechoslovakia called the Sudetenland. Soviet hopes of joining Britain and France in an anti-fascist alliance were now fading. Meanwhile, in the Far East, fighting broke out between the Soviet Union and Japan on the border between Manchuria and Mongolia.

The Nazi–Soviet Pact

On 23 August 1939 Germany and the Soviet Union astonished the world by signing a non-aggression pact – an agreement not to fight each other if one of them went to war with other countries.

The pact also involved a secret deal which Stalin could not resist. The Soviet Union would receive half of Poland as well as Finland, Estonia and Latvia. For this the Soviet Union would supply oil and raw materials for Germany's war industries. The Soviet Union thus got back the territories lost at the end of the First World War. But who really got the best deal? This was Hitler's reaction on receiving a message from Stalin, agreeing to the pact:

Source 8

Albert Speer, *Inside the Third Reich*, 1970.

Hitler stared into space for a moment, flushed deeply, then banged on the table so that the glasses rattled and exclaimed in a voice breaking with excitement, 'I have them! I have them!' Seconds later he had regained control of himself. No one dared to ask any questions and the meal continued.

On 1 September 1939 Germany invaded Poland, causing Britain and France to declare war on Germany. The Second World War had begun. Japan left the Anti-Comintern Pact in disgust. A sudden victory in the war against Japan in Mongolia in mid-September allowed Soviet forces to follow the Germans into Poland to take their share of the country. Soviet military bases were soon set up in Latvia and Estonia. On 28 September Germany and the Soviet Union agreed to redivide Eastern Europe giving more of Poland to Germany and Lithuania to the Soviet Union. But it was soon clear that Germany and the Soviet Union were nervous of each other.

Questions

1 Study Sources 1 and 2. How do they help explain the Soviet Union's fear of isolation?

2 Study Sources 3, 4, 6 and 7. Which of these sources suggest it was astonishing that the Soviet Union signed a non-aggression pact with Germany and which do not? Explain your answer.

3 For what reasons do you think Stalin made the non-aggression pact with Hitler?

4 How do you explain Hitler's reaction in Source 8?

6.4 The war to save the Fatherland

Stalin's plans went horribly wrong. Within two years of signing the non-aggression pact with Germany the Soviet Union was plunged into a desperate war for survival. This section examines what went wrong, and what saved the Soviet Union from defeat.

What went wrong?

Stalin hoped the Nazi–Soviet Pact would give the Soviet Union a breathing space while Germany went to war with France and Britain. This would give the Soviet Union time to ensure victory against Japan in the Far East and to prepare for war in the West. Time was also needed to finish reorganising the Soviet armed forces after the purges of their officers in 1937.

Hitler, on the other hand, knew that for a while Germany was safe from attack by the Soviet Union. Also the Soviet Union had promised to supply Germany with oil, iron ore, grain and other materials. With unexpected ease Germany took over Denmark, most of Norway, France, Belgium and Holland in 1940.

Operation Barbarossa

The Nazi–Soviet Pact was a marriage of convenience. By the end of 1940 Hitler had decided to end it. At dawn on 22 June 1941 an armed force of 3 million Germans suddenly flung itself on the Soviet Union. Operation Barbarossa (Red Beard) had begun. The result was devastating (Source 1).

The German air force achieved superiority in the air by destroying 1,200 Russian warplanes before they could leave the ground. Along a front of more than 1,600 kilometres the German

Source 1

The German advance into the Soviet Union and turning points in the war, 1941–1945.

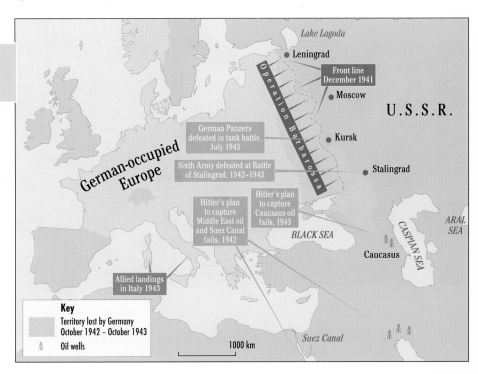

armies swept forward at the rate of 80 kilometres a day. By October 1941 the Germans were in sight of Moscow and Leningrad.

What saved the Soviet Union from defeat?

Many things saved the Soviet Union from defeat by Germany. The rest of this section outlines eight of them. When you have read about them, decide which were the most important.

The weather

It began to pour with rain in October 1941. This slowed the German advance as roads turned into rivers of mud. Most German vehicles had wheels instead of tracks. Then in November the temperature dropped and it began to snow. It was a record-breaking winter. Without anti-freeze, vehicle radiators froze. Temperatures reached –35°C. Heels and toes in German jackboots were the first to suffer.

Information from spies

A spy, Richard Sorge, told Stalin that the Japanese would not attack Russia in the Far East. This made it possible to transfer half of the Red Army, backed by 1,000 tanks and 1,000 aircraft, to defend Moscow. These tough Siberian soldiers were used to winters like this. They wore leather boots two sizes too big so that they could be stuffed with paper to help keep out the cold.

Source 2

A *Partisan's Mother* painted by S. Gerasimov.

Source 3

The Siege of Leningrad: a man and a woman, weakened by hunger, drag the body of their small child to be buried.

The heroism of the Soviet people

This can be illustrated by two scenes from the war. One is a painting (Source 2) which remembers the bravery of resistance fighters (partisans). The other is a photograph of a couple taking the body of their child for burial during the Siege of Leningrad (Source 3).

Partisans showed considerable courage. They ambushed and murdered Germans, acted as spies, and blew up bridges and railway lines in occupied territory to disrupt German supplies. Though they could hide in the forests, they depended on their villages to support them.

The German blockade trapped 3 million people in Leningrad. For 900 days from the end of August 1941 to January 1944 the Germans pounded the city with shellfire for nine hours each day. The shells killed 200,000 people.

The city's power stations ran out of coal just as winter set in. Water supplies froze. Without electricity the trams stopped running. In mid-winter there are eighteen hours of darkness in Leningrad. Temperatures dropped to as low as –40°C. People froze in unlit houses, burning their books and furniture to keep warm for as long as they could. As food became scarce, people started eating cats, dogs, mice, crows, vaseline, hair oil, and glue scraped from wallpaper – anything to stay alive. Some 630,000 people died of cold and hunger.

Source 4

Stalingrad at the end of the five month long Battle of Stalingrad (23 August 1942 - 31 January 1943).

Mistakes made by Hitler

Hitler's obsession with winning the Battle of Stalingrad resulted in a humiliating defeat for Germany and a psychological boost to the Soviet forces. Source 4 shows what was left of Stalingrad after the battle. A British war correspondent reported:

Source 5

Quoted in G. Hughes and S. Welfare, *The Red Empire*, 1990.

> Every inch of Stalingrad was a battlefield. For five months it had been a mincing machine .... walking over the frozen tortured earth you felt you were treading on human flesh and bones. And sometimes it was literally true.

Superior technology

The Soviet KV and T34 tanks had already proved superior to the German Mark III and IV. They played an important part in the greatest tank battle of all time at Kursk on 4 July 1943. The defeat of the Germans was a turning point in the war (Source 1).

Organisation by the Communist Party

Factories converted from making things like children's bicycles and typewriters to making flame throwers, guns and ammunition. The Communist Party brilliantly organised the evacuation of 1,500 whole factories and businesses from western parts of the Soviet Union to the Urals and Siberia by the end of 1941. Some 10 million people went with them. Within a week of the last pieces arriving, aircraft factories were turning out fighter planes. Within a year there was no shortage of planes, tanks, guns and ammunition.

Stalin's leadership

The number of Soviet deaths in the Second World War was 40 times greater than that of Britain and 70 times greater than that of the United States of America. It is thought that 27 to 28 million Soviet people died during the war. Many are believed to have died unnecessarily because of mistakes made by Stalin. Criticism of Stalin as a war leader can be seen in Source 6. It shows how the artist, Pytor Belov, remembers Stalin as war leader.

Stalin was quick and ruthless enough to replace useless army leaders like Voroshilov with more able men like Zhukov. To help these men and other officers, he ended the interference of Political Commissars in the armed forces. Despite terrible mistakes which cost the lives of thousands of Soviet people, he kept his nerve.

Stalin also avoided the mistakes of Tsar Nicholas in 1914 by letting civilian experts help organise supplies at the very beginning of the war instead of leaving this to the army. To do this he set up the State Defence Committee (GKO). To run the armed forces he set up a Supreme Command (STAVKA). His excellent memory and experience made him an able leader of both.

Source 6

A comment by Pytor Belov on Stalin as a war leader: millions swept into the path of German tanks in 1941.

Help from the Allies

From the moment the Germans invaded the Soviet Union the Americans sent massive quantities of aid to the Soviet Union as part of a deal with Britain called Lend-Lease: jeeps and lorries provided vital transport. Other valuable items were army boots, field telephones, tinned food and medicines. After Japan bombed the United States naval base at Pearl Harbor on 7 December 1941, the Americans became directly involved in the fighting.

However, Stalin accused the Western Allies of not playing a large enough part in the fight against Germany to take the pressure off the Soviet Union. It was only when the British and Americans landed in Sicily in the summer of 1943 that Hitler was forced to withdraw troops from the Soviet Union in order to help Italy.

Questions

1 The sub-headings on pages 90–92 show eight reasons why the Soviet Union was saved from defeat. Make a list of them.

2 Label those reasons which you consider most important 'A', those you consider the next most important 'B' and those you consider least important 'C'. Now explain your choice.

6.5   From Hot War to Cold War

The alliance between the Soviet Union and the Western Powers during the Second World War was an alliance between enemies. They made it to defeat a greater enemy: the alliance of Germany, Italy and Japan. The war transformed the balance of power in the world leaving two superpowers: the United States and the Soviet Union. For the next 45 years the two superpowers competed with each other in a 'Cold War' to dominate the world. A new weapon made this rivalry extremely dangerous: the nuclear bomb. The final section of this unit shows how the Soviet Union became involved in a Cold War against its former allies.

How did the Soviet Union get into a Cold War?

In August 1945 the Americans dropped two atomic bombs on Japan. The Japanese surrendered. Resistance fighters in China, Korea and Indo-China chased the Japanese out of their countries. The strongest of the resistance fighters were Communists. In the northern part of Indo-China they took control of the government. Communists also took control in North Korea (1947) and in China (1949).

Communists also made gains in Europe in the years after the war. The Americans believed that all Communists were controlled by the Soviet Union. So to contain the spread of Communism in Europe in 1947, the Americans not only sent economic aid to sixteen European countries but also guaranteed military assistance to any nation threatened by the spread of Communism.

The Berlin blockade
Communism spread to the East European countries with the help of the Soviet Union. These included East Germany along with the eastern half of Berlin. Stalin's distrust of the West, and his determination to make the Germans pay heavily for the damage caused by the war, almost led to war in Europe in 1948. Angered by Western money pouring into the British, French and American zones in West Berlin, Stalin tried to blockade the roads and railway lines passing through Soviet-controlled East Germany to Berlin. The Western Powers responded by a massive airlift of supplies which by 1949 defeated the blockade.

The Soviet atomic bomb
In the autumn of 1949 the Soviet armed forces produced their own atomic bomb. This shocked the Americans who thought it

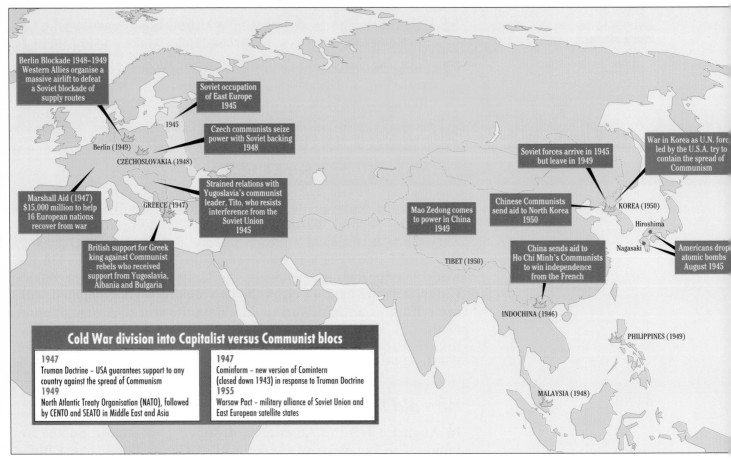

Cold War division into Capitalist versus Communist blocs

1947	1947
Truman Doctrine – USA guarantees support to any country against the spread of Communism	Cominform – new version of Comintern (closed down 1943) in response to Truman Doctrine
1949	1955
North Atlantic Treaty Organisation (NATO), followed by CENTO and SEATO in Middle East and Asia	Warsaw Pact – military alliance of Soviet Union and East European satellite states

Source 1

Flashpoints in the early stages of the 'Cold War' 1945-53

would take years for the Soviets to develop an atomic bomb. The Americans reacted by starting work on the hydrogen bomb. The American President Truman and his advisers now believed:

Source 2

National Security Council Document 68, 1950.

It is quite clear from Soviet theory and practice that the Kremlin* seeks to bring the free world under its dominion by the methods of the Cold War.

'**Kremlin** The ancient fortified centre of Moscow to which the Soviet government moved in 1918 from St Petersburg.

The Korean War, 1950–53

Soviet forces occupied North Korea in 1945; American forces occupied the South. The Soviet Union backed a Communist government in the North led by Kim Il Sung, whereas the Americans backed a government led by Syngman Rhee in the South. Unable to unite the country, Soviet and American forces left Korea divided at the 38th parallel (line of latitude). However, the North Koreans invaded the South in June 1950. To the American President Truman this was part of the Soviet Union's plan to spread Communism and so he persuaded the United Nations to come to the aid of the South. When UN forces led by General MacArthur chased the North Koreans back across the 38th parallel, the Chinese Communists came to their assistance. MacArthur prepared to drop atomic bombs. He later said:

Source 3

Quoted in Halliday and Cummings, *Korea*, 1989.

I would have dropped between thirty and forty atomic bombs ... strung across the neck of Manchuria ... [and] spread behind us a belt of radioactive cobalt, from the Sea of Japan to the Yellow Sea.

He wrote in a letter to an American politician which was read out in the House of Congress:

Source 4

Quoted in Trumbull Higgins, *Korea and the Fall of MacArthur,* 1960.

If we lose this war to Communism in Asia the fall of Europe is inevitable.

The British Prime Minister, Clement Attlee, and other world leaders became very alarmed. President Truman sacked MacArthur for going too far. Nevertheless, a vicious war continued until July 1953, causing over 20,000 casualties.

Questions

Compare Sources 2, 3 and 4.

1 Suggest reasons for the attitude of the US National Security Council and MacArthur towards the Soviet Union.

2 Why should historians take this evidence seriously when looking for an explanation of the Soviet Union's fear and distrust of the United States in the 1950s?

Review

1 Compare Sources 1 and 2 on pages 82 and 83. What changes would an artist have to make to update the painting (Source 2) in 1939?

2 Look at Source 1 on page 84. This painting shows Lenin meeting Eastern leaders.
  a What do you think the purpose of this painting might have been?
  b Why do you think the leaders of the Red Army (Trotsky) and the secret police (Dzerzhinsky) are in the picture?

3 What threat to the unity of the Soviet Union came from the different religions and nationalities in the Soviet Union?

4 In what senses were the Nazi–Soviet Pact of 1939 and the wartime alliance between the Soviet Union and the Western Powers both marriages of convenience?

5 Look at Sources 2, 3, 4 and 6 in Unit 6.4 (pages 89–93).
  a What different kinds of information do they give about how the Soviet peoples experienced the war?
  b What are the weaknesses of these sources as historical evidence of how the war was experienced?

Unit 7 • The legacies of Stalin and Khrushchev

7.1 Stalin's last years

Source 1

The celebrations of Stalin's 70th birthday in Red Square in Moscow in 1949. Notice how his image has been projected on to a hot-air balloon so that he seems suspended in the sky.

ОГОНЁК
№ 52   ДЕКАБРЬ   1949
ИЗДАТЕЛЬСТВО «ПРАВДА»

At first sight victory in war made Stalin's rule of the Soviet Union stronger than ever. This is what one schoolboy thought of him:

Source 2

Pavel Litvinov, interview for Thames television, 1990.

Stalin was like God for us. We just believed he was an absolutely perfect individual, and he lived somewhere in the Kremlin, a light always in his window, and he was thinking about us, about each of us .... For example, someone told me that Stalin could be the best surgeon. He could perform a brain operation better than anyone else, and I believed it.

Source 3

Moscow University. The 'wedding cake' style of architecture was used on several other buildings in the city.

Source 4

A Soviet cartoon commenting on the nine doctors' plot. The label on the hat in the water with the dollar sign says America and Britain. Who do you think are the people in the hat?

However, Stalin did not become any less repressive. The labour camps of the Gulag continued to fill as new purges began. The crime of many of the new victims was that they had allowed the Germans to capture them alive and make them prisoners of war. Stalin deported entire ethnic groups such as the Crimean Tartars to Central Asia and Kazakhstan for collaborating with the Germans.

The damage caused by the war was devastating. Stalin treated repair and reconstruction as an emergency. The aim of the Fourth Five Year Plan of 1946 was fast growth in all parts of the economy. There were severe punishments for those late for work, absent, or for anyone caught drunk. The last years of Stalin's life saw ambitious building projects. But, as Source 3 suggests, many of these projects seemed to have more to do with prestige and show rather than solving the very serious housing shortages.

Stalin continued to fear plots against him. He transferred high-ranking army officers like Marshal Zhukhov to less important posts and increased the Communist Party's control over the army. He promoted younger men like Leonid Brezhnev to weaken the power of the small circle of party leaders around him like Molotov, Beria, Malenkov and Khrushchev. He began a campaign against Jews. In January 1953 nine doctors were accused of being western agents and of murdering high-ranking Soviet leaders. Most of the doctors were Jewish (Source 4).

Those who survived being tortured were soon released. The reason for this was that on 5 March 1953 Stalin died of a stroke.

What problems did Stalin leave behind?

Stalin had turned the Soviet Union into a superpower much larger than the Empire of Tsar Nicholas. The cost was a dangerous Cold War. It was Stalin more than Lenin who had organised and expanded the Communist Party so that it could rule this empire. The result was a cruel dictatorship which moulded the careers of all the future leaders of the Soviet Union.

Economic and social problems

Collectivisation had not solved food shortages. One reason for this was that Stalin had placed faith in a scientist called Trofim Lysenko who fooled people into thinking that the harvest of crops could be increased by what he called 'vernalisation'. This meant soaking seeds at a certain temperature for a period of time before sowing. It was typical of the fear of Stalin that not even scientists who knew better dared challenge Lysenko.

Central control of economic planning stifled local initiatives to sort out problems in industry. Fear of punishment for not meeting production quotas led to 'fiddling the books' and making deals with a poorly paid workforce. This often led to short cuts, inefficiency and poor quality products. Concentration on industries which produced metals, electricity and chemicals meant shortages of consumer goods.

In the Ukraine, Belorussia and much of the European part of the Russia alone 25 million people lost their homes in the war. A serious housing shortage meant sharing homes with relatives, causing tensions in most Soviet families. The large number of men killed during the war left millions of women without husbands and millions of children without fathers. Middle-aged and elderly women (*babushki* or grandmothers) looked after children so that single mothers could work.

Source 5

Lavrenti Beria, who took over from Yezhov as Chief of the Security. Police (NKVD). It is rumoured that he delayed immediate medical treatment of Stalin after his stroke.

A police state

Stalin left an empire in which people did not feel protected by the law. They lived in fear of informers, the Security Police, a knock on the door at night and sentence to a labour camp for not being careful about what they said.

Everyone had to have an internal passport and a *propiska* (a dwelling permit). Those who lived in Moscow could get the best jobs, best education, go to the better shops, find food more easily and possibly come into contact with foreigners. Other cities and towns which provided jobs in high-technology, military or space industries had a high status. The passport system restricted access to these cities. Those who lived and worked on collective farms did not have passports except for men doing compulsory military service. The only other escape route was by getting a place at a higher education college or university.

Strict censorship meant that people were still supposed only to enjoy books, art, music and plays which expressed 'socialist realism' (see pages 75–76). However, the Russian Orthodox Church still hung on to the freedoms Stalin had given back to it during the war in 1953.

The news of Stalin's death and of the arrest and execution of Beria (Source 5), soon reached the Gulag camps. Kengir was one of many camps where the prisoners (*zeks*) turned on their former guards. Armoured tanks moved in to stop the revolt. Women linked arms and walked towards them. According to an eye-witness:

Source 6

Quoted in Geoffrey Hosking, *A History of the Soviet Union*, 1989.

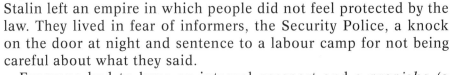

We thought the tanks would halt .... But no, they accelerated. Carrying out Moscow's orders, they drove straight over the live bodies. There were no cries: all we heard was a horrible sound of bodies being crushed and cracking bones.

Questions

1 Look at Sources 1 and 2. How do you explain such attitudes towards Stalin?

2 What appear to have been Stalin's aims after the war?

3 Why do you think Stalin continued to fear plots against him?

4 What questions would you ask a Russian who lived through this period (1945–1953) to find evidence that the Soviet Union experienced a 'cruel dictatorship'?

7.2   Nikita Khrushchev – de-Stalinisation?

Source 1

Nikita Khrushchev (1894–1971)

Khrushchev rose to power as an active supporter of Stalin. However, once in power he caused a sensation by denouncing Stalin. Then he began to 'de-Stalinise' the Soviet Union by reducing the cruelty of his dictatorship. He also cautiously allowed greater freedom to certain groups of people like artists. This section describes Khrushchev's rise to power and asks how far his reforms went to removing the shadow of Stalin.

Khrushchev's rise to power

Khrushchev began his working life as a fitter mending coal-mining machinery in the mines of the Donbass in the Ukraine. He joined and fought for the Bolsheviks in the civil war. Afterwards, he rose through the ranks of the party with the help of Stalin's ruthless ally, Kaganovich, who was in charge of collectivisation in the Ukraine. In order to move to the capital he persuaded the Ukrainian party to send him to Moscow to study for technical qualifications at the Industrial Academy. However, he took his career in the party more seriously than student life. Between 1934 and 1939 he was leader of the Moscow Communist Party. Khrushchev's enthusiastic support of Stalin's purges earned him a place in the government as well as the Politburo.

Source 2

A painting in typical socialist realism style which shows the cult of Stalin as a hero in 1950. To his right are Malenkov, Kaganovich and Beria; to his left Voroshilov, Molotov, Mikoyan and Khrushchev.

Khrushchev achieved an impressive war record. He helped organise the dismantling and movement of factories to the east and played a part in the Soviet victory at the Battle of Stalingrad. Stalin made him Prime Minister of the Ukraine in 1944. Then he brought him back to Moscow in 1949 and promoted him to reduce the growing power of Malenkov. Khrushchev became one of a group of five who replaced the old supporters of Stalin (Source 2). When Stalin died in 1953, the group of five agreed to form a collective leadership. But they feared that Beria planned to seize power for himself. Khrushchev plotted with Bulganin and Malenkov to have Beria arrested and shot. Khrushchev then used his control of the Communist Party, as First Secretary, to push Malenkov and Bulganin aside and become both Prime Minister and party leader.

How far did Khrushchev allow greater freedom?

De-Stalinisation
In 1956 Khrushchev invited top party officials to listen in secret to a speech. However, what he said was soon known all over the world and it caused a sensation. He told his listeners about how Lenin's last wishes to remove Stalin had been kept secret (see pages 65–66) and that:

Source 3

Khrushchev's speech to a secret session of the Twentieth Congress of the Communist Party, 25 February 1956.

Stalin originated the concept 'enemy of the people' .... This term made possible the usage of the most cruel repression ..... Facts prove that many abuses were made on Stalin's orders without consulting norms of party and Soviet legality .... The wilfulness of Stalin showed itself not only in the decisions concerning the internal life of the country, but also in the international relations of the Soviet Union ....

The release of millions of political prisoners from the camps followed this speech. But were these the words of a reformer who wanted to change the system he had helped to create? The camps and the dictatorship of the Communist Party remained.

■ What details of this speech would have caused a sensation and why?

1957: attempted coup
Khrushchev's secret speech stirred up trouble in Poland and Hungary and frightened senior members of the party. Rivals like Malenkov and supporters of Stalin like Molotov and Kaganovich tried to remove him from power in 1957. The attempted coup failed because Khrushchev had been careful to promote his younger supporters like Leonid Brezhnev to powerful positions in the party. He also had the support of the army led by Zhukhov, and of the new security force, the KGB.

■ How might Stalin have treated the plotters who tried to overthrow Khrushchev in 1957?

A sign of new times was the way Khrushchev punished the plotters. He gave Molotov the job of Soviet Ambassador to Mongolia, made Malenkov director of a power station, and Kaganovich director of an industrial plant in the Urals.

Writers and artists

The death of Stalin led people to hope that there would be greater freedom to express their views and to criticise conditions in the Soviet Union.

Ilya Ehrenburg had published a novel in 1954 called *The Thaw* which bravely suggested that a new era was beginning after the icy rule of Stalin. Banned authors like Bulgakov and Dostoyevsky could now be read.

Khrushchev did not discourage this, but did he approve?

Several writers and artists put him to the test. Vladimir Dudintsev's novel, *Not By Bread Alone*, which appeared in 1956, was about a lone scientist fighting for a better future against enemies who included factory managers and party officials. Khrushchev did not approve and fiercely criticised Dudintsev. Probably Khrushchev was frightened by the reaction to his speech in Poland and Hungary where it sparked off rebellions against Soviet rule. In 1957 he invited writers to his *dacha* (house in the country) outside Moscow and warned them that the party would not tolerate such literature.

The writer Boris Pasternak soon discovered the limits of the Party's tolerance. His new novel, *Dr Zhivago*, was greeted with outrage when it was published in Italy in 1957. A love story beginning during the 1917 Revolution and ending in Stalin's time, it contained passages such as Source 4:

Source 4

Boris Pasternak, *Dr Zhivago*, 1957.

One day Lara went out and did not come back. She must have been arrested in the street, as so often happened in those days, and she died or vanished somewhere, forgotten as a nameless number on a list which was afterwards mislaid, in one of the innumerable mixed women's concentration camps in the north.

Source 5

Khrushchev's gravestone.

Vicious criticism by the Party and government followed, causing Pasternak to turn down the Nobel prize for literature the next year. He died a broken man.

It was five years before Khrushchev allowed Alexander Solzhenitsyn to publish his novel, *One Day in the Life of Ivan Denisovich*, which described the life of a prisoner in one of Stalin's concentration camps.

Khrushchev, like Stalin, was suspicious of modern art. When he saw the work of the sculptor, Ernst Neizvetstny, he swore and said that a donkey could do better with his tail. But this was not the end of the story. Source 5 shows Khrushchev's gravestone. The artist had the courage to argue back. Khrushchev left instructions in his will that Neizvetstny should design his gravestone.

Religion

In 1943 Stalin had relaxed the ban on the Russian Orthodox Church but Khrushchev persecuted the Churches. He closed down 10,000 churches and most of the remaining monasteries. The KGB harassed pilgrims and monks. Some monks were beaten up and sent to psychiatric hospitals. Khrushchev also made life difficult for Evangelical Christians and Baptists.

Questions

1 Find information in this section which can be used as evidence that Khruschev **(i)** did, **(ii)** did not allow the Soviet people greater freedom.

2 Suggest reasons why Khrushchev was so cautious about giving greater freedom to writers and artists.

7.3 Economic and social policies

Khrushchev aimed to increase food production and improve the living conditions of the Soviet peoples. However, his policies for achieving these aims were deeply unpopular. The storm of criticism which they aroused helped to bring about his downfall.

Why were Khrushchev's policies so unpopular?

The Virgin Lands Scheme

Khrushchev took a keen interest in farming. The harvest of 1953 was very bad. His first answer to the problem was to merge collectives into larger units. Then in 1954 Khrushchev won support for a plan to plough 13 million hectares (an area greater than the size of England) of virgin land in North Kazakhstan to grow 20 million tonnes of grain. He put Leonid Brezhnev in charge of the scheme.

The scheme was a spectacular success at first. The 1956 harvests were especially good. However, an ecological disaster followed. Failure to rotate crops and to use fertilisers to feed the earth caused soil erosion. Windstorms between 1960 and 1965 ruined or damaged almost half the virgin lands. Harvests were so bad that in 1963 it was necessary to buy large amounts of grain from the United States and Canada.

Khrushchev's other solution to the food shortage was to force peasants to grow maize to feed livestock. He boasted that the Soviet Union would soon overtake America in producing meat, milk and butter. By 1962 maize covered 37 million hectares. However, the climate only allowed 7 million hectares to be harvested in a ripe condition.

Industry

The economy under Stalin was a command economy: the government in Moscow set targets, gave orders and punished failure. It seemed that the Five Year Plan of 1956–1960 would continue this. But in 1957 Khrushchev tried to transfer control of economic decision making to the republics of the Soviet Union. Over 100 Councils of the National Economy (*Sovnarkhozy*) replaced central economic ministries. Only ministries to do with defence remained under central government control. This upset those members of the central government who now lost responsibility and became less powerful. Khrushchev made more enemies.

He now replaced the Five Year Plan with a Seven Year Plan to last from 1958 to 1965. It aimed to expand the chemical industry, develop hydro-carbons, oil and natural gas, and to accelerate the space race. Production targets were too ambitious and not met. In 1961 Khrushchev restored the death penalty for economic crimes such as sabotage and fraud.

By 1964 the rate of growth of the whole Soviet economy had fallen to the lowest since the war. Critics grumbled that Khrushchev had made too many changes and that few people now knew how to do jobs properly. However, a look at some statistics gives a different impression:

Source 1

Based on A. Nove, *An Economic History of the USSR*, 1969, and Soviet sources.

Grain harvest in millions of tonnes

1953	82.5	1956	125.0	1959	119.5
1954	85.6	1957	102.0	1960	125.5
1955	103.7	1958	134.7	1965	121.1

Source 2

Based on A. Nove, *An Economic History of the USSR*, 1969, and Soviet sources.

Industry	1955	1965
Oil (million tonnes)	170	507
Coal (million tonnes)	390	578
Iron (million tonnes)	33.3	66.2
Electricity (billions of kW)	170	507
Tractors (thousands)	163	355

Social policies

The Soviet Union was short of skilled manual workers. Khrushchev's answer was that all children should leave school at 15 and work for two years. They could pass the exams needed for higher education by going to night school. The idea did not work. Young people lost the habit of study and employers soon found that young people's behaviour at work was no more mature than in school. More popular was the setting up of schools which specialised in subjects like languages, arts, sciences and mathematics, and ballet.

■ What do the statistics in Source 1 suggest about Khrushchev's economic achievements?

One of the aims of the 1917 Revolution had been to give equal opportunities to women. In 1956 maternity leave was increased to 112 days and there were more generous family allowances. Better social security benefits helped the large number of one-parent families and invalids caused by the war. However, there was a serious shortage of men because so many had been killed in the Second World War. Even by 1959, for every 1,000 women between the ages of 35 and 44 there were only 633 men. This caused a fall in the birth rate which lasted into the 1970s.

Source 3

A comparison of living standards in the USSR and USA (units per thousand population). *History of the 20th Century*, Purnell.

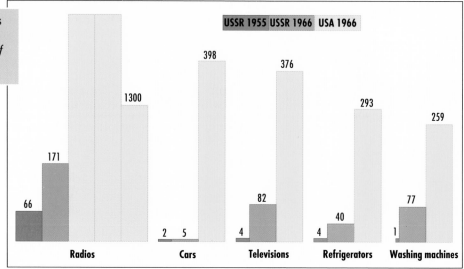

More than any Soviet leader before him, Khrushchev visited other countries. In 1959 Soviet cinema audiences watched a long documentary of his tour in the United States. How did their standard of living compare with that of the Americans? Source 3 gives some answers.

Khrushchev made a serious attempt to improve housing:

Source 4

Housing (million square metres) *Narodnoe Khozyaistvo SSR 1922–1987.*

1946–1950 (Fourth Five Year Plan)	200.9
1951–1955 (Fifth Five Year Plan)	240.5
1956–1960	474.1
1961–1965	490.6

Questions

1 Was the Virgin Lands Scheme a success or failure? Explain your answer.

2 Why did Khrushchev's reforms in industry make him more enemies?

3 In what way do Sources 1 and 2 give a better impression of Khrushchev's achievements than the rate of growth of the economy in 1964 which was the lowest since the Second World War?

4 **a** Look at Source 3. In what ways did living standards in the Soviet Union improve between 1955 and 1966?
b How did they compare with the USA in 1966?

5 Look at Source 4. How did the rate of growth in housing in the last years of Stalin compare with that of the years Khrushchev was in power?

7.4 Khrushchev's downfall

Criticism of Khrushchev's reforms in the Soviet Union and a growing unease with his handling of foreign relations led to his downfall. This section looks at aspects of Khrushchev's foreign relations which attracted criticism.

Why did Khrushchev's handling of foreign relations help cause his downfall?

Eastern Europe

The Second World War left much of Eastern Europe under Soviet control. In 1955 the Soviet Union tightened its control over Albania, Bulgaria, Czechoslovakia, East Germany, Hungary, Poland and Romania by making them join a military alliance under Soviet command, the Warsaw Pact. Only Yugoslavia, led by Tito, stood up to the Soviet Union. Khrushchev's solution to this problem was to meet Tito and accept that Yugoslavia had a right not to follow the Soviet model of Communism.

Khrushchev's speech in 1956 criticising Stalin (see page 100) sparked off rebellions in Poland and Hungary where people hoped that the Soviet Union would now give them independence. Khrushchev responded by brutally crushing the rebellion in Hungary but by allowing the Polish leader, Gomulka, to stay in power provided that he allowed the Soviet Union to control him like a puppet. Meanwhile, East Germans began to see East Berlin as an escape route from Soviet rule to the West. To stop a flood of refugees, including professional and skilled people, Khrushchev ordered a wall to be built to divide East from West Berlin in 1961.

Source 1

Many spy novels and films were set against the background of the Cold War. This photo comes from the film *The Ipcress File*, based on the novel by Len Deighton.

Movement to and from Eastern Berlin was carefully controlled through gates with names like 'Checkpoint Charlie'. Secrecy, excitement, fear and spying became a part of the spine-chilling atmosphere of the Cold War which inspired novels and films in the West (Source 1).

The Far East
The Communist leaders of China strongly criticised Khrushchev's attack on Stalin. Khrushchev refused to give the Chinese the technical knowledge to build nuclear weapons. The Soviet Union's support for India in a border war with China in 1962 worsened already bad relations between China and the Soviet Union.

The space race
The Soviet Union became the world leader in science and technology by launching two space satellites, Sputnik I and Sputnik II, in 1957 (Source 2). This was the first important step in an expensive competition with the USA. The USA feared wrongly that the USSR now had the technology to launch long-range ballistic missiles. Khrushchev took delight in encouraging the hero worship of Yuri Gagarin who made the first human space flight in 1961.

Nuclear weapons
While Khrushchev boasted about the technical achievements of the Soviet Union, he also showed signs of wanting to end the expensive and dangerous arms race. How serious was he? Source 3 is a Soviet anti-bomb poster which appeared in 1958. In that year the USA rejected a peace treaty proposed by the Soviet Union to ban nuclear weapons from Germany, but volunteered to suspend the testing of nuclear weapons.

Peaceful coexistence
In 1959 Khrushchev still appeared to want a thaw in the Cold War when he said:

Source 2

Cartoon by Vicky in the *Daily Mirror*, 20 December 1957.

Source 3

A Soviet anti-bomb poster, 1958

Source 4

In our day there are only two ways, peaceful coexistence or the most destructive war in history. There is no third way.

A speech by Khrushchev in 1959

Spy planes
However, the idea of peaceful coexistence took a blow in 1960 when the Soviets shot down an American spy plane over Soviet territory and captured the pilot, Gary Powers. Eisenhower, the United States President, offended the Soviet Union by refusing to apologise.

Khrushchev's style
Khrushchev's aggressive and crude style sometimes caused embarrassment in the foreign relations of the Soviet Union. Look at Source 5. In September 1960 Khrushchev attended the United

Source 5

Khrushchev at the United Nations in 1960 where he loudly interrupted speeches and banged a shoe on the table (he was wearing shoes on both feet at the time). How would you feel if the leader of your country behaved like this?

Nations General Assembly where he banged a shoe on the table in protest at Western interference in the affairs of Third World countries like the Congo (Zaire) and Cuba. This behaviour shocked Soviet viewers who did not think it was how a statesman should behave.

The Cuban Missiles Crisis

The final straw came over Khrushchev's clash with the new young United States President, J.F. Kennedy. He forced the Soviet Union to dismantle nuclear missile launching bases in Cuba. This was deeply humiliating.

Khrushchev's overthrow

In 1964 Brezhnev plotted with Podgorny, Suslov and Kosygin to overthrow Khrushchev. Among the methods he suggested were the use of poison, a plane crash or a car accident. Instead they made Khrushchev retire on health grounds and gave him a pension and a *dacha* (house in the country). Khrushchev later commented:

Source 6

R. Medvedev, *Khrushchev*, 1982.

... perhaps the most important thing I did was just this – that they were able to get rid of me simply by voting, whereas Stalin would have had them all arrested.

Questions

1. Source 1 shows a spy from the West being led off to torture by East German guards. What does it suggest Westerners thought of the Soviet Union during the Cold War?

2. Study Source 2. Which events in 1957 help explain these pictures?

3. What tensions in foreign affairs help to explain the Soviet anti-bomb poster (Source 3)?

4. What do you think Khrushchev meant by 'peaceful coexistence' in Source 4?

5. a Give examples of Khrushchev's handling of foreign affairs which attracted criticism from inside the Soviet Union.
   b Did Krushchev strengthen or weaken the image of the Soviet Union as a world superpower? Explain your answer.

Review

1 Looking back on his career what might Khrushchev have said were the high points and the low points?

2 What part did Khrushchev's policies play in his downfall in 1964:
(i) inside the Soviet Union?
(ii) in foreign relations?

3 Read Khrushchev's self-assessment in Source 6 (page 107). Write down which of the following comments you most agree with and explain why:
(i) Khrushchev was too modest about his achievements.
(ii) Khrushchev was right to be modest because in the end he failed.

4 Below is a checklist to compare the state in which Stalin and Khrushchev left the Soviet Union. Copy the table and in each box put a mark out of ten and add up each score.

	Stalin	Khrushchev
1 How much did the Soviet people respect Stalin and Khrushchev?	☐	☐
2 How serious were the economic and social problems of the Soviet Union?	☐	☐
3 How much freedom did the Soviet people have?	☐	☐
4 Had relations with other countries improved?	☐	☐
	Total ☐	Total ☐

b Explain the difference or similarity of the total scores.

Unit 8 • After Khrushchev – for better or worse

Source 1

Russian dolls bought at a Moscow street market in 1991.

Source 2

A portrait showing Brezhnev displaying his medals.

Look at Source 1. These dolls were on sale in a Moscow street market in 1991. They are a political version of a Russian doll – a favourite souvenir. The dolls fit inside each other and represent Lenin and his successors(right to left). Look at dolls 2 and 3. What is each holding which helps to show that these dolls are Stalin and Khrushchev? Dolls 4 and 5 were the two most important leaders after Khrushchev – Leonid Brezhnev and Mikhail Gorbachev. What did each achieve for the Soviet Union?

Leonid Brezhnev

Leonid Brezhnev ruled the Soviet Union from 1964 to 1982. At first he shared power with others who had helped overthrow Khrushchev. But by 1971 he was the most important leader in the Soviet Union. In 1977 he made himself Chairman of the Presidium of the Supreme Soviet – the first leader of the USSR to be both party leader and head of the government. He encouraged a 'personality cult' of himself, similar to the cult of Stalin. This could be seen in portraits of Brezhnev like that shown in Source 2.

In the first years of his rule Brezhnev followed a tough foreign policy and cracked down on any signs of communist neighbours, like Czechoslovakia, breaking away from control by the Soviet Union (Source 3).

Inside the Soviet Union Brezhnev took an equally hard line against dissidents – scientists and writers like Andrei Sakharov and Alexander Solzehinitsyn who openly criticised communist rule for failing to respect human rights.

By contrast in the years 1969 to 1974 Brezhnev tried to ease tensions in the Cold War because the Soviet Union badly needed Western technology, grain and money to develop the economy. This led to a détente or relaxation in tension over Eastern Europe. The détente years saw a big rise in the standard of living inside the Soviet Union.

However, Brezhnev's decision to invade Afghanistan in 1979 shattered détente. Look at doll 4 on page 109. It shows Brezhnev wearing medals and holding a bottle of vodka. These clues refer to the last years of his rule. These were years of stagnation in the economy and growing social problems of alcoholism, drug abuse and crime. His own love of drink, flattery and of being awarded medals became a source of jokes. During the last two years of his life crippling illnesses reduced him to a figurehead surrounded by other older men in poor health. It was said that the Soviet Union was run from the geriatric ward of the Kremlin.

Source 3

Protesters defying and trying to set alight Soviet tanks after the invasion of Czechoslovakia in 1968

Mikhail Gorbachev

A much younger man, Mikhail Gorbachev, emerged as the next leader of the Soviet Union after Brezhnev. Doll 5 in Source 1 shows him holding a book containing his ideas for change, *perestroika* (which means restructuring or renewal) but not an end to Communism. He put a stop to the Cold War, gave dissidents like Andrei Sakharov their freedom, tolerated religion and showed greater respect for human rights.

Like Khrushchev, Gorbachev took the opportunity to travel, and enjoyed walkabouts to meet and talk to crowds of people (Source 4). His wife, Raisa (see doll 5 in Source 1) travelled with him on trips at home and abroad and became very popular. People in the Soviet Union worried about her influence over Gorbachev and the expense of her wardrobe.

Perestroika failed to solve the desperate economic problems of the Soviet economy (Source 5). Greater openness (*glasnost*)

Source 4

Gorbachev on a 'walkabout' with Raisa.

encouraged more criticism and demonstrations by peoples who wanted to leave the Soviet Union (Source 6). To try to win their support Gorbachev ended dictatorship by the Communist Party

Source 5

A Moscow queue outside a supermarket, March 1991.

Source 6

Muslims demonstrating against Soviet rule in Azerbaijan in 1989.

and allowed other parties to take part in elections. This was more than conservative communist leaders could stand. In August 1991 they tried to overthrow Gorbachev in a coup d'etat. An old political rival, Boris Yeltsin, rallied support to rescue him and arrest the plotters. Yeltsin then forced Gorbachev to ban the Communist Party altogether. Gorbachev resigned as leader. The Soviet Union ceased to exist and the Empire fell apart. Was this for better or worse? Has the break up of the Soviet Union improved the lives of its people?

Source 7

Front page headline from the *Sunday Times*, 25 August 1991.

Gorbachev destroys Communist party in new Russian revolution

Source 8

Map showing the economic resources shared by the USSR.

Questions

1 Look at Source 1.
  a Give the names of each of the five dolls.
  b Describe and explain the meaning of the clues on dolls 2 and 3.
  c Which of Sources 2 or 3 match the clues on dolls 4 and 5? Why?
  d What other information helps to explain the clues on dolls 4 and 5?

2 **a** What changes did Gorbachev try to bring to the Soviet Union?
  b Suggest reasons for making these changes.
  c Look at Sources 5, 6 and 7. What link is there between each of these sources and Gorbachev's downfall in August 1991?

3 **a** Why do you think the Soviet Union broke up when communist rule ended?
  b What does Source 8 suggest were the economic disadvantages of the Soviet Union breaking up?

Review

1 'Life under communist rule was an improvement on life under Tsarist rule.' List the arguments for and against this view.

2 Imagine you are in a hot-air balloon with Tsar Nicholas, Lenin, Stalin, Khrushchev, Brezhnev, Gorbachev and Yeltsin. You are losing height and will crash unless you throw out four of these people. Who will you choose to throw out? Why?

3 Has the break up of the Soviet Union been for better or worse? Give reasons for your answer.